GENERATION

# EX-

CHRISTIAN

WHY YOUNG ADULTS ARE LEAVING
THE FAITH...
AND HOW TO BRING THEM BACK

DREW DYCK

MOODY PUBLISHERS
CHICAGO

Edited by Elizabeth Cody Newenhuyse
Interior design: Ragont Design
Cover design: Faceout Studio
Cover and interior image: Shutterstock, #20346466 and Faceout Studio;
                    Steve Gardner/PixelWorks Studios, Inc.

Library of Congress Cataloging-in-Publication Data

Dyck, Drew.
    Generation ex-Christian : why young adults are leaving the faith—and how to bring them back / Drew Dyck.
        p. cm.
    Includes bibliographical references.
    ISBN 978-0-8024-4355-7
    1. Ex-church members. 2. Church work with ex-church members.
3. Young adults—Religious life. I. Title.
    BV4921.3.D93 2010
    248.2'4—dc22
                                                            2010018806

We hope you enjoy this book from Moody Publishers. Our goal is to provide high-quality, thought-provoking books and products that connect truth to your real needs and challenges. For more information on other books and products written and produced from a biblical perspective, go to www.moodypublishers.com or write to:

Moody Publishers
820 N. LaSalle Boulevard
Chicago, IL 60610

1 3 5 7 9 10 8 6 4 2

*Printed in the United States of America*

To my wife, Grace.
You were aptly named, my darling.
I love you.

# Contents

# Foreword

There has been a pressing need for a book to identify why so many young adults are abandoning the faith and to provide a road map for how Christians should respond. *Generation Ex-Christian* is that book.

As an educator, author, and speaker, I have the privilege of speaking to thousands of young people each year. Some young Christians understand their faith and can defend it well. Unfortunately, most cannot. As a result, when these young Christians leave home—and their belief in God comes under fire—many leave the faith as well. That's why I'm passionate about teaching apologetics to youth—to equip them to reach others and withstand the inevitable assaults on their faith.

Drew's book is for the ones who have fallen under the barrage. In the following pages, you'll encounter young people who have wandered away from God. Drew probes their experiences and helps us understand the various dynamics that led to their departures. But he doesn't leave us there. He offers insightful ways to connect with these young "leavers," engage them in life-changing conversations about God, and ultimately lead them home. For the sake of the next generation, I urge you to read, study, and put the principles of this book into practice.

There has been much discussion recently about youth abandoning the faith, but *Generation Ex-Christian* is the first research-based book to thoroughly explain why they're leaving. Drew has done a marvelous job of capturing the hearts and minds of young people who have walked away. And he provides a hopeful remedy for what we can do about it. After reading this book, you'll be equipped and inspired to lead young people back into the arms of their heavenly Father.

SEAN MCDOWELL

General Editor of *Apologetics for a New Generation*

# Introduction

The shepherd is on his knees.

He leans precariously over a cliff. With one arm he steadies himself with a staff. With the other, he reaches down to a sheep stranded on a jutting rock below.

This image comes from *The Lost Sheep*, by Alfred Soord. The painting invokes a familiar story. It's Jesus' parable of the shepherd who leaves the ninety-nine sheep to search for the one that has wandered away.

It's a strange story. The shepherd's math is off, his actions incomprehensible. And like any good love story, it's a desperate one, a tale of stubborn, sacrificial love. The shepherd will go to any length to bring his lost sheep safely back to the fold. Every time I read the parable or see the painting, I'm moved. I wonder if there's a better image to illustrate God's desire to reach those who wander from Him.

Today the landscape is dotted with lost sheep. Young people are defecting from the faith at an historic rate. Over the following pages, we'll meet dozens of young people who have wandered from God. They are part of what researchers call *Generation Y* or the *Millennials*, the name given to those born after 1980. Some are slightly older—like me, they were born in the late 1970s. In some cases, names and details have been changed to protect people's privacy, but the stories are true.

As we delve into the lives of these young ex-Christians, we'll look for patterns that will help us engage them. No two leavers are identical, but upon close observation some categories emerge. We will meet six different kinds of leavers (the postmodernist, the recoiler, the modernist, the neo-pagan, the rebel, and the drifter) and look at practical ways to connect with each type.

This book is about lost sheep. But it's also about the Good Shepherd. Watching a loved one abandon the faith is heart-wrenching. Those of us familiar with this painful experience need to remember that the Good Shepherd cares. He has more invested in our loved ones than we do, and He too longs for their safe return. As you pursue the lost sheep in your life, watch for the Good Shepherd's footsteps. He leads the way. And He's already searching . . .

# Section I

## Postmodern Leavers

# 1— Good-bye, God

My friend Abe was raised as a Christian, but abandoned his faith during college.

"I don't know what happened," he said with a shrug. "I just left it."

When I heard about Abe's "deconversion," my mind jumped to the last time I'd seen him. It was at a Promise Keepers rally the year after we graduated from high school. I remember being surprised to see him there; neither of us had been strong Christians in school. But watching him standing next to his father in the coliseum, it was clear something had clicked. As the voices of twenty thousand men lifted in unison, Abe squeezed his eyes shut and extended one slender arm skyward. He seemed solemn yet peaceful, totally absorbed in God's presence.

It was a powerful evening. I can still hear the words of one of the event's speakers. He wasn't the most eloquent in the lineup, and he had a slight speech impediment, but his passion for Christ was palpable.

"I don't know about you guys," he said. "But I want to

run the race so hard that when I reach the end, I fall exhausted into the arms of Jesus."

After he spoke, the stadium was silent. In that moment I think we all felt the same way. We didn't want to just hobble through our spiritual journeys. We wanted to sprint. When we came to the end, we wanted to collapse into the arms of Jesus.

I'd considered myself a Christian ever since my dad walked into my room one night in 1983, knelt beside my lower bunk, and led me in the sinner's prayer. I was five years old when that happened and probably didn't understand exactly what I was saying. And yet, it was real. It wasn't until my late teens, however, when I carefully read the gospels, that the faith truly became my own.

When I saw Abe worshiping at the rally, I assumed he had undergone a similar transformation. We were both pastors' kids. We had both gone through the proverbial rebellious phase, but that didn't mean we didn't believe.

## How could the guy I'd watched lost in worship turn cold toward God?

That's why I was shocked by his decision to leave the faith. I was a little curious too. What had prompted Abe, who was my age, and from a remarkably similar background, to defect? How could the guy I'd watched lost in worship turn cold toward God?

### EXODUS NOW

It's a question that's being asked a lot these days. Young adults are fleeing the faith in record numbers. Abe may be a riddle, but he's not rare.

Religious beliefs are elusive targets for conventional research. No survey or study can fully probe the heart of a person, much less the mind of God. So when it comes to assessing how many people are joining or leaving the faith, we're dealing with educated guesses. To steal the apostle Paul's beautiful phrase, "we see through a glass darkly."

Still a number of recent surveys give us important clues about the emerging generation's patterns of belief. And it's not a pretty picture. Among young adults, there's a major shift taking place— away from Christianity.

The first indicators are church attendance and involvement. Here the statistics are grim. According to Rainer Research 70 percent of youth leave church by the time they are twenty-two years old.[1] Barna Group estimates that 80 percent of those reared in the church will be "disengaged" by the time they are twenty-nine years old.[2] Unlike older church dropouts, these young "leavers" are unlikely to seek out alternative forms of Christian community, such as home churches and small groups. When they leave church, many leave the faith as well. One commentator put the reality in stark terms:

Imagine a group photo of all the students who come to your church (or live within your community of believers) in a typical year. Take a big fat marker and cross out three out of every four faces. That's the probable toll of spiritual disengagement as students navigate through their faith during the next two decades.[3]

I don't need a "big fat marker" to perform this experiment. I've watched it play out among my friends over the past decade. The social networking website Facebook has emerged as the younger generation's preferred way to communicate with large numbers of friends. It's a great way to keep tabs on people from the past. As I scan the online accounts of former youth group friends, the drift from God is unmistakable. Many no longer even wear the Christian label. Others have not explicitly renounced the faith, but their online pictures, comments, and profiles reveal lifestyles and attitudes few would describe as Christian. Some were particularly surprising to me. Under the "religious views" category in her profile, one previously devout Christian had simply written: "God has left the building." Another shock came from a sweet, soft-spoken girl who used to sing on my church's worship team. Now her album of pictures looked like an advertisement for *Girls Gone Wild*. She had sent me a message wanting to catch up. I wrote back and asked if she was "still into Jesus." Her response said it all—I didn't get one.

**As I scan the online accounts of former youth group friends, the drift from God is unmistakable.**

Of course Facebook accounts hardly serve as reliable gauges of spiritual health. When it comes to most of my friends, I probably won't discover where they are at in their relationships with God. I might not have the opportunity to see them again face-to-face, let alone delve into their most deeply held beliefs. Thankfully, I did have that opportunity with Abe.

## "I FELT NOTHING"

Fast-forward six years from that Promise Keepers rally and Abe's sitting in my studio apartment, slapping a cigarette from a pack of American Spirits. The intervening years had taken us each down very different paths. I was married. He was single. I was headed to seminary. He was wrapping up law school. I was an active Christian. He'd rejected the faith. At the time of his visit, he was celebrating a last stint of student-life freedom by motorbiking across the United States. I offered him my futon when he rolled into town. It wasn't much, but compared to the nights he'd been spending in his pop-up tent, it probably felt like the Marriott.

We talked late into the night. Since high school he'd lived an exciting and eclectic life. I felt a twinge of jealousy as he described experiences that seemed lifted from a Jack Kerouac novel. He had lived in London, and worked as a bartender. He backpacked through India. He spent summers tree planting in northern Alberta, a lucrative seasonal gig that funded his nomadic existence. Somewhere in Asia he suspended his travels to meditate in a Buddhist monastery. He'd become a vegetarian.

"I can't see how people can justify using animals as a resource," he said as he fried up a delicious feast of falafel balls for me and my wife.

His experiences had changed him—most significantly in his views about God. When I broached the subject, his voice grew quiet.

"When I left the faith, I thought it would feel really bad. I assumed I'd come right back. But I didn't feel bad. I felt nothing."

Though he was philosophical about his departure, he didn't regret it. In fact he felt liberated. And he was slightly combative.

"Can you honestly say that Christianity has been good for humanity?" he asked.

His tone was equally critical when he talked about his parents, especially his father whom he described as "a right-winger."

If I had been saddened by Abe's decision, his father was devastated. When he heard of Abe's decision, he rushed him the book *Mere Christianity* by C. S. Lewis, hoping it might bring him back.

It didn't.

Abe read the book, even enjoyed it, but didn't change his decision to bid his faith farewell.

"Growing up I had an uncle that wasn't a Christian and we prayed for him all the time," Abe said wistfully. "They probably pray for me like that now."

## A DIFFERENT UNIVERSE

Why do young people leave the faith?

Whenever I ask people inside the church I receive some variation of the same answer. They leave because of moral compromise, I am told. A teenage girl goes off to college and starts to party. A young man moves in with his girlfriend. Soon the conflict between their beliefs and behavior becomes unbearable. Something has to give. Tired of dealing with a guilty conscience and unwilling to abandon their sinful lifestyles, they drop their Christian commitment. They may cite intellectual skepticism or disappointments with the church, but don't be fooled. These are just excuses, smoke screens designed to hide their real reason for going astray. "They change their creed to match their conduct," as my parents would say.

There's even an academic basis for this explanation. Psychologists call this "cognitive dissonance." Basically the theory goes like this. Opposing beliefs or behaviors cause psychological distress. We seek to resolve the tension by dropping or modifying one of those contradictory beliefs or behaviors. Once we do, our psyche's harmony is restored.

I think there's a lot of truth to that hypothesis—more than most young leavers would care to admit (and we'll explore this reason for leaving later in the book). "The Christian ideal has not been tried and found wanting," wrote G. K. Chesterton. "It's been found difficult and left untried."[4] Even practicing Christians can attest to the truth encapsulated in that clever verbal twist. Living the Christian life is hard, and when you're falling short, as we all do, it's easy to forfeit relationship with an invisible deity in order to indulge sinful, real-world desires.

For Abe, I'm sure moral compromise played a role. Christian morality didn't exactly jibe with his new lifestyle, which included relationships with the opposite sex that fell outside the biblical model. It would have been difficult for him to hold a Christian worldview while engaging in a pattern of behavior that opposed it.

**I saw that his parents' attempts to call him back to God were futile because he inhabited a different universe.**

Yet the moral compromise explanation didn't tell the whole story. He had other reasons for leaving, and they weren't just smoke screens. The more we talked, the more I believed that they were at the root of why he left. He balked at Christian entanglement with conservative politics. He pointed out what he saw as a lack of compassion for the poor among Christians. And he wasn't moved by the apologetics of yesteryear. Ultimately I saw that his parents' attempts to call him back to God were futile because he inhabited a different universe, one populated with ideas and sensibilities that were completely alien to them. I'd soon begin to discover the laws of this new universe and find out just how many other young adults had followed Abe through the wormhole.

# 2- Reality Remix

Have you noticed a change in the way today's young people speak? No, I'm not referring to the ubiquitous and improper use of the word "like" or the annoying addition of texting acronyms such as "OMG," "BFF," and "LOL" to the popular lexicon. I'm talking about a way of speaking that suggests a subtle yet profound change in the way the younger generation actually processes reality.

Maybe you have heard young people talk about a different "truth" for each person, an idea that would have seemed absurd even fifty years ago. "True for you, but not for me," is a common refrain. Or maybe you've sensed the high premium the emerging generation places on individual experience.

The language used in regard to romantic relationships is especially telling. Recently I was watching a TV show popular with young adults. One of the characters was counseling a friend in a troubled marriage and urged him to get a divorce. The breakthrough came when he grabbed his beleaguered friend by the shoulders and said,

"You know that you haven't loved her (his wife) for a long time." This was supposed to be a good friend, delivering good advice.

The scene's implication was clear: staying in a relationship after feelings of love have fled is wrong. How you feel in a particular moment trumps any previously made commitments, including wedding vows. This way of thinking seems to permeate all aspects of morality: "Do whatever works for you," could be the mantra of many of today's young people.

Such statements may leave you scratching your head. Isn't truth by its very nature exclusive? And why is experience the end-all when it comes to morality? What if your experience leads you astray?

If you've noticed this type of language, you've detected the influence of a paradigm commonly called postmodernism.

## THE END OF REASON

With our bellies filled with falafel, Abe and I moved the few short feet from the kitchen to the living room. In reality, the presence of different rooms was an illusion, the work of imagination and clever furniture arrangement; the small apartment had no dividing walls. We put on some tea and plopped into my second-hand IKEA chairs. I leaned across the coffee table. I needed to understand how Abe dismissed the central claims of the Christian faith, claims that were so compelling to me.

The writing of C. S. Lewis had been a formative influence in my own journey. One of Lewis's most popular arguments is often referred to as the "liar, lunatic, or Lord" or "trilemma" argument. It is a response to the view that Jesus was merely a great moral teacher, but not the divine Son of God. Nonsense, says Lewis. If Jesus was not telling the truth about His identity, He was not a great moral teacher. To Lewis, there were only three possibilities about a man who claimed to be God. Either he was lying, crazy, or he was telling the truth. "You can shut Him up for a fool or you can fall at His feet and call Him Lord and God," Lewis writes. "But let us not come with any patronising nonsense about His being a great human teacher. He has not left that open to us. He did not intend to."[1]

How could Abe sidestep such a potent argument? What had he decided about Christ? In order to find out I began a line of questioning designed to steer him toward Lewis' trilemma trap.

"What do you think of Christ's ethics?" I asked him.

"Flawless," Abe conceded.

Now I have him cornered, I thought.

"Okay, then how do you deal with His claim to be God? How can someone with flawless ethics lie about his identity?"

Abe is educated, and he knows the Bible. I expected a sophisticated explanation for this apparent contradiction. Maybe he would attack the historicity of the gospels or challenge my traditional interpretation of them. I was ready for such objections. I wasn't ready for what he said.

> ## How could I reason with someone who didn't believe in reason?

"I don't really believe in all that rationality," he said. "Reason and logic come from the Western philosophical tradition. I don't think that's the only way to find truth."

His response silenced me. How could I reason with someone who didn't believe in reason? My interactions with Abe sent me on a quest to understand his worldview.

## SHIFTING GROUND

In the preface to his book, *Live to Tell: Evangelism for a Postmodern Age*, Brad Kallenberg recounts his decade-long stint as a college campus evangelist. When he started in the late 1970s, conversion rates were high. Kallenberg recalls that about 10 percent of gospel presentations resulted in conversion. But by 1985 the percentage rate had slipped to about 6 or 7 percent—this despite the fact that Kallenberg and fellow evangelists were working twice as hard to make the gospel intelligible to increasingly biblically illiterate students.

Disheartened by the dwindling numbers they switched tactics, investing money in huge on-campus advertising campaigns to generate a "warm market" of students. Despite such efforts, numbers continued to fall. Shortly after Kallenberg's departure from the ministry in 1989, the percentage of conversions fell to an abysmal 2 percent.

All along Kallenberg and the other campus evangelists were sharing the same message. The results, however, were changing dramatically. So what was happening? For Kallenberg the mystery cleared when he enrolled in graduate school and began studying philosophy. A major shift had taken place in the field, he discovered, that was now beginning to affect the culture. Suddenly Kallenberg understood why it felt like the "ground was shifting under (his) feet." The old ways of thinking were crumbling and Christian faith was regarded differently in the new milieu. Kallenberg discovered that he had been feeling the impact of postmodernism. And those were just the first tremors. The earthquake was still coming. By the 1990s, it had shaken Western culture to its core, changing the ideological landscape for an entire generation.

## BREAKING IT DOWN

Postmodernism is a word you hear a lot these days, but ask what it means and you'll likely get a blank stare—or a different definition each time you ask. There's good reason for the ambiguity. Postmodernism is not easy to define. And just when you think you have it pinned, it changes shape, taking on different meanings in various fields such as art, architecture, and philosophy.

Yet, as a worldview, postmodernism does have identifiable characteristics. The most succinct definition probably comes from the French philosopher Jean Lyotard, who famously defined postmodernism as "incredulity toward metanarratives." What does that mean? Basically that those big stories—the kind of overarching narratives by which we define reality—are regarded with suspicion. In a postmodern world, no one story is large enough to contain the whole of reality, much less define it for all people.

This suspicion of metanarratives has at least two important implications. First, it results in a radical redefinition of truth, reason, and reality. With no standard narrative to serve as a guide, reality, is determined by individual experience. And since there are an endless variety of stories, nothing can be absolutely true for everyone. According to philosopher J. P. Moreland, "On a postmodernist view, there is no such thing as objective truth, reality, value, reason and so forth." As I read this definition, Abe's words echoed in my ears. "I don't believe in all that rationality . . . I don't think that's the only way to find truth."

The postmodernist view holds that there is a different "truth" for each person. And experience—not rationality—is the key to finding that truth. It's easy to overstate this particular feature of postmodern thought. It's not that all postmodern thinkers completely negate truth (although some do). Rather they tend to find rationality and logic odd players in the spiritual arena. In their private lives, they may be thoroughgoing modernists. After all, most postmodernists aren't shy about reaping the fruits of modernity: they ride airplanes, use cell phones, and embrace science. But often a different set of rules applies to their spiritual and moral lives. Many of these otherwise intelligent, educated people will consult psychics and espouse reincarnation. It's not spirituality or even supernatural claims with which they have a problem. Broad proclamations of truth are not frowned upon just because they stretch credulity; they're condemned because they're seen as arrogant and dangerous. Rick Richardson, InterVarsity Christian Fellowship's national field director for evangelism, observes of the postmodern crowd: "When people ask questions about homosexuality, for instance, we're tempted to think they're asking questions about right and wrong. But they're not. They're asking about dominance and oppression."[2]

At one point in our conversation Abe made an important clarification. It wasn't that he was specifically opposed to Christianity, he said. He was against any form of moral absolutism. To Abe, any belief held too strongly was dangerous. People who were too sure of their beliefs were apt to force them on others. His distaste for moral absolutes placed him firmly in the postmodern camp.

A second feature of postmodern thought comes from a movement in philosophy and literary criticism called "deconstructionism." It's natural to assume that deconstruction would mean the opposite of construction, to tear something down. And in fact, that's exactly how the word is usually used. Originally, however, this coinage of the enigmatic French philosopher Jacques Derrida referred primarily to a way of interpreting literary texts. To deconstruct a literary text is to expose its contradictions and oppositions, to demonstrate that it can ultimately have no fixed meaning. For Derrida, language's constructed and self-referential nature makes its correspondence with the outside world tenuous at best, hence his famous dictum: "There is nothing outside the text."

The reason I explain such an arcane term is because Derrida's thinking did not stay confined to the ivory towers of academia. Upon Derrida's death in 2004, *Washington Post* reporter Patricia Sullivan wrote, "'Deconstruction' has become one of the few terms that, like 'existential' a generation or two earlier, has escaped from dense philosophical and literary papers to pepper modern culture, from movie reviews to government policy pronouncements."[3] Those who took up Derrida's mantle in the culture were not content merely to apply his theories to literary texts. Deconstruction quickly became an approach to all areas of life. As a result it has engendered a radical skepticism about the credibility of truth claims and raised suspicion toward traditional beliefs.

A third precept of postmodernism is more positive: concern for the marginalized. That's one beef postmodern thinkers have with metanarratives, or big stories—they tend to neglect the "little people." Talk to postmodern thinkers about the wisdom of the Greeks, and they'll remind you that the Greeks held slaves and subjugated women. Bring up the founding fathers of the United States and they'll talk about the cruel conquest of the natives. Christian faith comes under fire too. For many postmodern thinkers the historical horrors of the Crusades and Inquisition cast a pall over the Gospel message. Andy Crouch writes, "Many streams of postmodern thought are animated by the desire to do justice to the claims of those whom the dominant culture has excluded."[4] As Abe talked about Christians who were indifferent to the poor and disenfranchised, he was giving voice to one of the central tenets of postmodern thought.

Postmodernism has been the subject of countless Christian conferences and books. Some see it as an enemy of the church. Others regard it as a savior. I fall somewhere in the middle. Postmodernism is not the bogeyman, but it's no angel either. Certain aspects of postmodernism do align with Christian beliefs. One can hardly open the Bible without seeing God's concern for the poor and lowly. Christ championed the cause of marginalized people and even linked His identity to the lowly (Matthew 25:45). Catholic theologians remind us of God's "preferential option for the poor." The book of James stipulates that pure religion is attending to the needs of widows and orphans (1:27). Yet other dimensions of postmodernism—such as moral relativism and a low view of truth—are clearly irreconcilable with a biblical worldview.

Our concern here, however, is not to come to a conclusive opinion about postmodernism. We simply want to understand its impact on the culture and learn how to speak meaningfully to those under its sway. Fortunately, as we'll see in the next chapter, there are many creative ways to do just that.

# 3 — Welcoming Back Postmodern Leavers

W hen I heard of Abe's deconversion, the phenome-non of apostasy was not altogether new to me. Growing up, I was reminded of the possibility almost daily as we prayed for my wayward uncle, Bob. He had grown up a Christian but later rejected the idea of God alto-gether, becoming the only one of my father's nine siblings to leave the Christian faith. Despite our persistent prayers, Uncle Bob showed no signs of softening. I remember, when I was fifteen years old, discovering an atheist tract he had surreptitiously slipped between the pages of my Student Bible during a visit. It was entitled "20 Reasons Why the Bible Is NOT the Word of God." I remember only one of the reasons, perhaps for its strangeness: it held that Ecclesiastes' teaching that "There is nothing new under the sun" was proven wrong by the 1969 moon land-ing. "So there's nothing new under the sun?" the pam-phlet read triumphantly. "How many men walked on the moon before 1969?!"

Our prayers for Uncle Bob seemed to go unanswered.

It wasn't a test of my faith, but it did tax my resolve. Was it really worth praying for someone who remained so closed off to God? To my knowledge, my uncle never came around. He collapsed and died of a heart attack, ironically in the lobby of a church. I still don't know why he was in a church or why, when his wife reached him, he had a look of surrender and peace in his eyes. Perhaps in that final moment, he breathed a prayer of contrition? Only God knows. I miss my uncle, and I remember how strange it felt to stop praying for him so suddenly. Somehow though, hearing of grownup leavers never presented a challenge to my burgeoning faith. I was always delivered tidy—and probably oversimplified—explanations for why they left.

## STRANGERS FROM OUR MIDST

Watching members of my generation leave, however, has been different. It's especially sad and unnerving to witness people I've grown up with abandon the faith. I had encountered a smattering of leavers by accident, enough to alert me to the troubling trend. But when I put the word out that I was writing this book, the floodgates opened. Almost immediately I was inundated by people wanting to talk. Most were strangers, people I'd been connected to through friends of friends. Others were people from my past: a woman who'd gone to my youth group, an old basketball buddy who confessed that he doesn't consider himself a Christian anymore, and many others.

As I read up on the topic I learned that evidence of the trend is not merely anecdotal. Research shows that this generation has a strong tendency to fall away. In *UnChristian*, David Kinnaman relays his findings from thousands of interviews with young adults on the topic of Christian faith. Though Kinnaman focuses on the beliefs of outsiders (not those who leave the faith per se), he found that most young people have had broad exposure to Christianity. In fact, 65 percent of all American young people report making a commitment to Jesus Christ at some point in their lives. Yet, based on his surveys, Kinnaman concludes that only about 3 percent of these young adults have a biblical worldview.

> **65 percent of all American young people report making a commitment to Jesus Christ at some point in their lives.**

Kinnaman translates the percentages into real numbers: "This means that out of the ninety-five million Americans who are ages eighteen to forty-one, about sixty million say they have already made a commitment to Jesus that is still important; however, only about three million of them have a biblical worldview."[1]

Of course that doesn't mean that there are 57 million young leavers in the country. Only the most theologically lax would count anyone that makes a pledge or says a prayer as a genuine disciple of Jesus. On the other side of the coin, not having a biblical worldview doesn't seal your fate as an unbeliever. Like I wrote earlier, ultimately the precise number of young adults leaving is beyond human knowing. Still, such research shows us something very valuable about young people outside the faith. As Kinnaman concludes, "the vast majority of outsiders in this country, particularly among young generations, are actually *de*-churched individuals."[2]

In other words these are not strangers, some mysterious denizens of a heathen underworld. Rather most unbelieving outsiders are old friends, yesterday's worshipers, children who once prayed to Jesus, even if they didn't fully grasp what they were saying. Strictly speaking, they are not an "unreached people group." They are our brothers, sisters, sons and daughters, and our friends. They have dwelt among us.

**Most unbelieving outsiders are old friends, yesterday's worshipers, children who once prayed to Jesus.**

Encountering these leavers has forced me to ask some tough questions about how I live and present my faith. When it comes to postmodern leavers, the question of approach is especially vexing. Appeals to logic and reason are clearly inadequate. There are no airtight arguments, I've realized, to persuade them to return to the faith. So how can they be reached? What kinds of words and actions might resonate with them?

## TALKING TO POSTMODERN LEAVERS

I wish I could finish Abe's story with a climactic tale of return. I'd love to recount how he decided to give God another chance, or at least agreed to reexamine the faith. Unfortunately the most I can say at this point is that Abe is still on a journey. Yet I was encouraged (and surprised) by a comment he made toward the end of our discussion. In true postmodern fashion he shrugged his shoulders and mused, "Who knows, maybe I'll come back (to faith) some day."

Thinking back over our conversation, I realize that I made some missteps. Actually, that's an understatement; it was more like an adventure in what *not* to say to a postmodern thinker. I needled him with arguments. I tried to force him into a logical corner.

I brought up C. S. Lewis, the patron saint of traditional apologists. Talking to leavers with a postmodern worldview can be frustrating, particularly for those with a more traditional mindset. In a cruel twist of irony, thorough preparation can actually sabotage effectiveness. You have your arguments ready, your facts straight, and you want to put them to good use. You stand "prepared to give an answer to everyone who asks you to give the reason for the hope that you have" (1 Peter 3:15 NIV). But then you talk to postmodern thinkers and find that everything you've studied seems useless. They're not interested in philosophical proofs for God's existence or in the case for the resurrection. Your best defenses of the faith seem to fall on deaf ears, or worse yet, make them even more resistant to your message.

What follows are some tips I've discovered—often by falling flat on my face!—about how to speak meaningfully to this tough-to-reach group of young adults.

## TELL YOUR STORY

In a postmodern world, metanarratives are suspect, but personal perspectives are sacrosanct. Whatever you experience or feel deeply will be respected. You are authorized to tell your story. TV Thomas, a Malaysian evangelist, who speaks on university campuses all over the world, told me, "Young people might say, 'don't tell me anything about Christianity.' But they don't mind you telling them your story, because it's *your* story."

Your story is the account of how you came to Christ, or it could simply be a description of what Jesus means in your everyday life. In evangelical parlance, we often call such stories "testimonies." Unfortunately over the years the testimony has calcified into a veritable genre, a formalized way of sharing the origins of faith within a Christian context. As a result, today many testimonies are rote scripts, complete with predictable plot points: Life was empty and miserable. But then, in a mountaintop moment, salvation came. Since that experience life has been happy and full of meaning.

Don't get me wrong—for some, this reflects their experience of coming to faith. For most, however, it does not. Pre-Christian lives are not categorically miserable, nor are our conversion experiences always climactic. In fact, many report a gradual, even painful, process of coming to Christ. And the Christian life is decidedly not easy or consistently euphoric. Indeed for some of history's great saints, following the Carpenter from Nazareth has meant donning their own crown of thorns.

When telling your story to postmodern leavers, it's especially crucial to avoid slipping into the traditional "testimony" rut. Remember, you're speaking with people who have likely heard dozens of testimonies. They know the formula well. And they can tell when you're adapting your experience to fit the mold. They will be far more impressed with transparency. Be honest with them about your struggles, even your doubts. In the end they'll respond more favorably if they can see that you're not so different from them.

**Sometimes we feel the need to project an ironclad certitude when talking about our faith.**

Many of the postmodern leavers I talked to felt like Christians don't have an appreciation for the nuances of reality. They complained that Christians offer easy answers to complex questions. I don't think Christians are simplistic thinkers. But I think that sometimes we feel the need to project an ironclad certitude when talking about our faith. Unfortunately, that approach backfires, especially for leavers who have been nurtured in a deconstructed world, where the contradictions and complexity of life loom large.

## RE-ENCHANT THE GOSPEL

I have a Christian friend in Los Angeles who told me that he was growing frustrated trying to share his faith.

"People are nice to me," he said. "They just don't listen."

He had talked with a coworker who even thanked him. "I'm so glad you found something that makes you happy. Thanks for sharing. I'm glad that works for you."

My friend was encountering postmodernists and discovering the hard way that, in a postmodern environment, your personal experience might have little or no bearing on another person's life. That's why you need to move from the mini-narrative of your personal story to the metanarrative of the cosmic gospel.

But be sure to sidestep the land mines of the postmodern terrain. Avoid arguing for the legitimacy of the gospel based on reason and science. Remember the Four Spiritual Laws, the popular evangelistic tract created by Campus Crusade founder Bill Bright in the early 1960s? Just imagine how the tract would read through the eyes of a postmodern person. It employs the language of science. The tract begins, "Just as there are physical laws that govern the physical universe, so are there spiritual laws that govern your relationship with God."[3] The pamphlet is also heavy on propositions (stand-alone belief statements) and light on story. It appeals primarily to logic and concludes with a standardized salvation prayer. I'm not picking on the Four Spiritual Laws; it was an excellent tool for its time. But for a postmodern audience, it is virtually obsolete. Any similar approach you take with postmodern leavers will be met with cynicism or indifference. Based on his research of young adults, Kinnaman writes, "Even if you are able to weave a compelling logical argument, young people will nod, smile, and ignore you."[4]

Instead, aim to convey the gospel story in creative and beautiful ways. Retell stories that show Jesus' heart for the marginalized, such as His exchange with the woman at the well, His healing of lepers, or the story of Him rescuing the woman caught in adultery. Leavers already know the basic gospel outline. But as I interviewed them about their impressions of Christian faith, I started to see that what many of them had in mind was a distortion, a faded image of the vivid Messiah encountered on the pages of Scripture. They desperately need passionate storytellers willing to re-enchant the gospel story, and let the person of Jesus capture their imaginations afresh.

## BUILD TRUST

C. S. Lewis's style of apologetics may not resonate with a postmodern generation. But when it came to interacting with those who leave the faith, the Oxford don offers some sage advice. "A person must court a virgin differently than a divorcée," said Lewis. "One welcomes the charming words; the other needs a demonstration of love to overcome inbuilt skepticism."[5]

This principle holds especially true for postmodern leavers. Don Everts and Doug Schaupp, "missionaries to the college campus in the United States" with InterVarsity Christian Fellowship, have been fortunate enough to witness literally thousands of postmoderns come to Christ. Throughout their two decades in ministry, they began to notice some common steps along the postmodern path to faith. "As we celebrated all the conversions we had witnessed, the same themes were popping up again and again."[6] The first step Everts and Schaupp identified among people that came to the faith: learning to trust Christians.

What most of our friends have told us is that the process of coming to faith really gained traction for them once they started to significantly trust a Christian. There is an invisible wall between distrust and trust—a threshold. It seems that people must move through this threshold into trust in order for them to continue on to Jesus.[7]

### "I feel like Christians aren't interested in being my friend. I wish they'd just like me for me."

As I interviewed postmodern leavers, the issue of trust came up over and over again. "I feel like Christians aren't interested in being my friend. I wish they'd just like me for me. They just want to preach at me." The postmodern leavers in your life will not respond to your message unless you truly love and accept them, regardless of where they stand spiritually. Befriend them unconditionally. Show genuine interest and love.

## INVITE THEM TO SERVE

Postmoderns prefer to discover truth through experience rather than reason. Most also have a strong social conscience and a willingness to serve the poor and oppressed. You can honor these admirable characteristics by inviting them to participate in service projects with you and other Christians. This provides a natural access point for them to the church and actually allows them to participate in the work of God in the world. Traditional evangelism has required belief before belonging, but there's no reason why that order can't be reversed. I'm not saying that proper beliefs aren't important. They are. But Jesus Himself extended the simple invitation to His disciples, "Follow Me," knowing that the full truth of His identity would be revealed only as they walked beside Him. We'd be wise to do the same. Of course, it may be inappropriate to invite outsiders to engage in certain church activities that are reserved for those with committed beliefs, but there are plenty of opportunities to enlist their help with humanitarian projects.

Daniel Hill, a young Chicago-area pastor who took a part-time job at Starbucks to reach postmoderns with the gospel, advocates this approach. "There are lots of ways to invite someone to experience Jesus besides attending a church service," he says. "One of the most powerful of these opportunities is when we invite friends to discover God's heart for the poor, disadvantaged, and oppressed."[8] For Hill, inviting young postmoderns to serve allows him to circumvent their initial apprehension about conventional church.

> These experiences are often reserved for the already-convinced in church life, but we emphasize that many times a Post-Christian's problem is with church, not with the activities of a Jesus-follower . . . if our Post-Christian friend declines an invitation to church, this isn't the end of the road in our spiritual friendship.[9]

Indeed, as many churches can attest, inviting postmoderns to participate in acts of service often marks the beginning of a journey that leads to a new life in Christ.

## FOLLOW THE LEADER

There was someone who did all these things quite well—Jesus! Think about it. He earned people's trust through service and sacrifice. He invited people to serve alongside Him. He preferred colorful stories over linear arguments, to sketch a compelling picture of God's radical, beautiful kingdom. We'd do well to surrender our often clunky and predictable methods to follow Him, moving from soul to soul, whetting spiritual appetites, speaking the lost language of spiritual longing, challenging, probing, provoking, baffling. It's not an easy act to follow. But it's worth it. As we follow Jesus in this way, we'll be surprised at how many others join us on the journey.

# Portrait of a
## POSTMODERN LEAVER

Mike wasn't comfortable with labels.

"The categories are bull," he said, when asked if he considered himself a Christian. This was more than a trivial objection; it was integral to his worldview.

"That's the problem," he said. "People start thinking that categories are reality. That kind of thinking is part of what explains my spiritual homelessness."

When pressed about his spiritual status, he offered a reluctant reply. "If anything, I'd describe myself as Hindu. I wouldn't say Christianity is false. I just wouldn't say that it's any truer than anyone else's story. Some people want proof that God's on their side. But where I'm at now, I don't need that. My position rings true to me and enough folks I know that it is proven true by my experience."

This position is a far cry from where Mike was only years ago. He and his wife both graduated from the evangelical school Biola University, traveled as part of a worship band, and even helped plant two churches in California.

They also became involved with emergent village, a

movement among younger evangelicals disillusioned with traditional forms of church. Mike and his wife were heavily influenced by the book *A New Kind of Christian* by popular emerging church author Brian McLaren. Mike described the book as "hugely life-giving." In the short term their involvement with emergent served as a boon to their faith, "the thing that kept us in the Christian camp." Yet Mike also described the movement as the path that led them away.

"I felt like me and some of the others in that conversation started pushing against the edges of the tradition, even against the authority of the J-man (Jesus).

"Here we were, touring with a worship band, and my wife is reading a book by the Dalai Lama. And we start asking questions like, 'What if truth has been in multiple places at multiple times?'"

Mike still admires Jesus, but now views Him differently. "I believe He was a son of God. He was a very unique avatar, to use a Hindu term. I think He was one of those people who embodied God at a certain time and place. I'd say He's very similar to the Buddha."

Suddenly Mike pauses to acknowledge a "twinge of guilt" about comparing Jesus with Buddha. "That's probably because I spent so much time in the evangelical world. But it seems so unimaginative to say that there's only one way. With Christians, if the J-man didn't say it, they aren't into it."

His departure from orthodox Christianity hasn't sat well with his evangelical family. "They have just been really confused by my path. I've tried to have conversations with them, but they don't go very well—at all! Now I'm just silent."

Mike still holds out hope for some sort of ultimate truth, and confesses that he's still on a journey.

"Gosh, I hope there's some sort of transcendent reality," he says. "I don't think it's probably a personal God, but I'm still working through that."

# Section 2

Recoilers

# 4- Into the Night

I love driving at night.

It's a passion I trace to childhood. My family couldn't afford to fly, but that didn't keep us from going on vacation. My three older brothers and I would stuff into the back of our family's station wagon and strike off, my mom's nose buried in a book and my dad behind the wheel. Leaving our home in central Alberta, Canada, we set out to visit my grandparents in Oregon or my uncle in California.

My dad didn't like to stop the car. Unless there was an exploding bladder or a fistfight in the backseat, we kept rolling. We usually planned to stay the night at a hotel, but once my dad got into the groove there was no stopping him. It saved money; besides, he preferred to drive in the cool hours of the evening and often right through the night.

Sometimes I would stay awake to keep him company. I would lean my head into the front seat and ask him questions about God. As we hurtled through the dark, surveying clusters of vivid stars that seemed just an arm's length beyond the windshield, the topic felt natural. I wasn't after answers. I wanted to revel in mystery. "Dad, why is the universe so big? And why does God care about us? We're so small."

He would smile and shake his head. "I don't know, Drew. It's amazing. It's just amazing."

I guess those were my first theological conversations.

My first memories of the Bible are equally pleasant. Every day, once my older brothers left for school, my mother and I had "cozy time" on the couch. "Cozy time" was just what it sounded like. We would cuddle, but as we did, my mom would read to me from a children's picture Bible. I can still see the book's depictions: a muscular Samson fighting the Philistines, a wizened Moses holding up the Ten Commandments, Jesus' luminous body emerging from the tomb. To this day, I think those pictures still color my perception (for better or for worse) of the stories in the Bible. My mom wasn't content to merely read the stories. She acted them out, and did the voices. She even provided the application. She'd point to the Bible characters on the pages.

"Some day, you'll be brave like King David . . . some day you'll be faithful like John."

I have little doubt that these early spiritual experiences have shaped the person that I am today. Is it really any surprise that I'm still a Christian? My parents did an excellent job of introducing me to the faith. Sure, they weren't perfect—no parents are. But they coupled knowledge of God with love and affirmation.

Of course, positive childhood associations are not adequate to ensure an abiding faith. I had pivotal experiences later in life that personalized and strengthened my faith. Fond memories are not enough. Yet I have no doubt that these formative encounters inclined my heart toward God and helped me weather the storms that would assail my faith in adolescence and early adulthood.

But that was my experience. Not everyone is so fortunate.

For some, knowledge of God comes with harsh words—for others, with black eyes. For many, retaining their faith means swimming upstream against a current of painful memories.

A lot of young people fall into this camp. Their negative childhood and teenage experiences are the primary reasons they have left the faith. They have suffered abuse and vowed that they would never take the chance to be victimized again. I've named these leavers "recoilers"—they withdraw from the faith because of the pain they have endured.

## HURT AND HARD

One such person is Katie. When she "friended" me on Facebook I had trouble recalling who she was. Really, I should have remembered. After all, we went to the same youth group for years. Our fathers were both pastors.

**For many, retaining their faith means swimming upstream against a current of painful memories.**

But maybe I wasn't entirely to blame. As a teenager Katie didn't exactly take pains to be noticed. She attended church sporadically, and always sat near the back. When she came to youth group events she seemed to hover on the periphery, her willowy frame disappearing under an oversized sweatshirt. The few times we talked she was either painfully shy or unnaturally giddy, a troubled kid.

When I sent out a general message looking for ex-Christians, she responded quickly.

"I'd be willing to talk to you."

When we spoke I was stunned to hear the transformation in her voice. The previously socially awkward and withdrawn girl was now a confident-sounding woman, pursuing advanced education in social work. She had pulled her life together, but it was a life that no longer included God.

"I don't go to church anymore," she stated. "I'm on the fence about God. I don't even know if He exists."

## LAST STRAWS

I knew about some of the painful things that had transpired in Katie's family. Her father had carried on affairs with multiple women at once. His immoral behavior cost him his marriage and ministry, despite his justification that the sexual relationships were part of his attempts to counsel the women with whom he was sleeping. As reprehensible as her father's philandering was, Katie, cited other reasons for leaving the faith.

"There were two big things that turned me off to Christianity," she said.

The first reason involved her mother. In the wake of her parents' divorce, her mother struck up a romance with a man in prison.

"She said that she loved him," Katie recalled with irritation. "I warned her that it wouldn't work out, but she didn't listen. She said 'Don't worry, God said He was blessing the relationship.'"

The romance proceeded smoothly—that is until the boyfriend was released from prison.

"He ended up doing the exact same things that got him into prison in the first place," said Katie. "My mother was devastated. Some kind of blessing that turned out to be!"

Her second reason for leaving the faith involved a single

incident that took place in our youth group, though I had no rec-ollection of it. The leader of the group, she recalled, had stated that the only reason to leave a marriage was infidelity. Katie took exception.

"What if my husband was beating me?"

The leader smiled. "Did your parents give you that?" he said.

For Katie the slight was still raw, more than ten years later.

"He acted as if a female couldn't think on her own," she said in disgust.

When Katie insisted that the question was her own, the leader obliged with an answer. "He said I would have to stay with my husband, and pray for him," Katie recalled.

That was not the response Katie was looking for. "I said to myself right there, *no way!*"

I could see why Katie was offended, but I had to wonder why these incidents had struck such a powerful chord. Yes, it would be upsetting to see your mother dive headlong into an ill-fated romance. And sure, the fact that her mother attributed her actions to God's leading must have been disillusioning for Katie. But still, it was her mother, not her. And I knew her mother. That was just how she talked. She attributed almost everything she did to the "leading of the Spirit."

Katie's reaction to the exchange with the youth leader left me similarly perplexed. Why would an implied insult and a hermeneu-tical quibble produce such a strong reaction? It was almost as if that single exchange had sounded the death knell for her faith. I couldn't fully understand why these experiences had so dramati-cally changed her spiritual trajectory. But further into the con-versation, other issues came to light. Suddenly her reactions made perfect sense.

## BEYOND INTELLECTUAL OBJECTIONS

The more I interviewed, the more I realized many left for distinctly psychological or emotional reasons. These kinds of leavers were far more difficult to find, however. Intellectual leavers tend to be more vocal and prolific. They attend meetings, and write angry online screeds against Christianity. Finding them is easy. Those who leave because they were hurt are often harder to locate. Rarely will they seek the opportunity to vocalize how they were hurt. Such confessions take courage and vulnerability, attributes in short supply among those subjected to psychological trauma.

**Many actually leave the faith for emotional reasons and find intellectual reasons to back it up.**

Besides, it sounds far more legitimate to leave on intellectual grounds than emotional ones. It doesn't sound very credible to say that you rejected God because someone hurt you in His name. It's much more respectable to cite intellectual incredulity. However, many actually leave the faith for emotional reasons and find intellectual reasons to back it up. The head follows the heart.

This tendency required that I carry a healthy dose of skepticism into my interviews. To understand why many young people had truly left meant reading beneath or even against their language. This was no easy task, and it was more art than science. For instance, one young woman told me she left Christianity because "it just isn't credible" and spent the better part of an hour detailing her significant intellectual objections. But as the conversation continued, something interesting came to light. She had attended a prominent Christian college, where she'd suffered a mental breakdown after feeling ostracized by the community and betrayed by Christian friends. The time line of her story was telling. It was shortly after this traumatic experience that she stopped practicing her faith. It was only in subsequent years that she constructed her elaborate system of doubt. Her intellectual doubts may have prevented her from returning to Christianity, but they were almost certainly not the reason she left in the first place.

## A HISTORY OF ABUSE

As my conversation with Katie continued, details of her tragic childhood came to light. She had been molested. Not just by one person, but by two, and both were members of the church she attended as a child. Worse yet, her parents had been partly to blame for one of the incidents. They left her with a babysitter whom they knew had molested before, naively thinking she wouldn't repeat the behavior.

Suddenly Katie's extreme reaction to the youth leader made much more sense. Considering what she'd endured, her response didn't seem extreme at all. The question Katie had posed to that youth leader was more than a hypothetical query. She'd been abused, and she wasn't about to let it happen again. "No way!" as she put it.

I also saw her response to her mother's romantic misfortunes in a new light. Katie's own abuse made her extra sensitive to her mother's heartache. The fact that her mother saw a divine promise, but ended up a victim, soured her view of God. It must have felt like reopening an old wound to Katie, who even as a teenager knew all too well the unfairness of life.

## "YOU'VE BECOME SO HARD"

Katie had other negative associations with church.

"I always felt like we came second to church people," Katie said.

During regular church meetings, Katie and her sisters were often relegated to the basement. "I don't blame my parents now," she said, "but at the time it felt like we weren't as important."

Although Katie stays away from church as an adult, her mother still occasionally pulls her into a church function. She told me about one such recent occasion. At the service, one of her mother's friends approached Katie with an intense look of concern on her face. She grabbed Katie by the shoulders.

"Katie, you've become so hard," she said.

Katie's voice faltered as she recalled the encounter. "That affected me," she said. "I don't want to be hard."

She paused to regain her poise.

"But you have to be hard. You have to be hard . . . or else life will hurt you."

# 5- Recoilers

Often the reasons recoilers reject faith reach back into early childhood. To understand them better, let's take a brief look at some basic principles of developmental psychology. Christian psychologist Marjorie Gunnoe explains that, from ages seven to eleven, children become extremely focused on the concept of fairness. This developmental stage has implications for a child's nascent theology. Gunnoe explains:

> Children automatically transfer this sense of fairness to God. They develop a strong intuitive sense that God is fair. So the relationship with God is based on reciprocity. If God doesn't answer a prayer it's because they didn't pray enough. If something bad happens to someone, it's because that person did something bad.[1]

Sooner or later, this basic sense of fairness is challenged.

"Something happens to the child that forces him or her to say 'I didn't deserve this.' Maybe it's a divorce, abuse or a tragedy—some event that's very jarring to their belief in the fairness of life," says Gunnoe.

The event will likely cause them to see God in a new light. "The degree to which this event is tangled up with theology, will determine how angry the child will become toward God. The stage is set for the child's foundation to be shaken."

This is a precarious moment. The child is confused and desperate for answers.

"If they are going to stay within the Christian camp, it's because someone is there to help them make sense of the event within a theological context," says Gunnoe. "They need someone to say, for example, 'The person who abused you was not being a good Christian.' This thing that the child intuitively knows is evil has to be labeled as evil."[2]

And what if it isn't labeled as evil? What happens if there's no one around to help the child make sense of the traumatic event?

"If abuse is not acknowledged, and it's being done in the name of God, eventually you're going to have some kind of break," says Gunnoe.

## DANGERS OF SANCTIFICATION

All traumatic events leave scars on the psyche, especially events suffered in childhood. Yet, as hurtful as such experiences are, they don't have to become obstacles to faith. In fact, many people with painful pasts actually gravitate to the church, perhaps drawn by the promise of love and healing.

Yet for some, hurtful experiences drive them from the fold—and then keep them away. But how can a history of abuse draw some to the church, while causing others to run from it? Why would it simultaneously attract and repel?

It all depends on the context in which these hurtful experiences occur. In theology, the word *sanctification* refers to the process of a Christian's spiritual growth. In the psychology of religion, however, the term takes on a different meaning. Psychologist Annette Mahoney defines sanctification as the "psychological process through which aspects of life are perceived by people as having spiritual character or significance." In other words, this kind of sanctification occurs when we see life through a spiritual lens.

Take marriage, for example. The dictionary defines it as "the state of being united to a person of the opposite sex as husband or wife in a consensual and contractual relationship recognized by law."[3] But as a Christian I see marriage as much more. I can't think of the institution separately from the Bible's description of marriage as a reflection of the relationship between Christ and His church. So, in psychological terms, I have sanctified marriage. Of course this is not a bad thing to do. Indeed, as Christians we are commanded to view our lives in the light of biblical reality. Sanctification also has enormous practical benefits. Research studies have demonstrated that people who sanctify aspects of their lives have less conflict and more satisfaction in marriage, are warmer and less verbally aggressive as parents, and possess greater coping skills when dealing with stress.[4]

However, there are potential dangers or risks to sanctification, including violence in the name of submission, failure to enact change (thinking that abuse has been sanctioned by God), and magnified psychological difficulties for victims of religious mentors. In other words, if we're not careful, seeing our lives through a spiritual or religious lens can lead to problems. We can either become abusers, overconfident in our actions, and buoyed by a false sense of divine license. Or we can be abused and fall prey to passivity or even internalize the abuse, thinking that God must approve of the evil being done in His name.

**For a child who suffers some form of "sanctified" abuse, the resulting spiritual damage can haunt that person for a lifetime.**

This is not to say that we shouldn't sanctify our lives. It only means that by doing so, we open ourselves up for greater damage if the relationships we sanctify become abusive or evil. Most adults can tease out the human elements from the divine, but children have greater difficulty making such distinctions. For a child who suffers some form of "sanctified" abuse, the resulting spiritual damage can haunt that person for a lifetime. Such is the case for many recoilers—they often have experienced some form of abuse in the name of God. A Sunday school teacher verbally hurt them. An elder molested them. Perhaps the abuse was even perpetrated by a member of their own family. One psychologist recounted reviewing dozens of case studies in which children were verbally and physically abused and beaten by their parents in extremely religious homes. "It's very difficult for those children to differentiate between God and their abusers. They usually end up throwing everything out. After all, the abuse they suffered was all done in God's name."[5]

Of course not every recoiler has undergone dramatic physical or verbal abuse. Some may have been wounded by a particularly judgmental and harsh Christian leader, or a religious person who belittled them. There's no shortage of garden-variety human failings that sour people on the faith. Social psychologist Julia Exline writes: "In the shadow of sensational crimes lurk ordinary ones that nonetheless do serious damage. Religious communities are not immune from the usual human tendencies toward gossip, greed, petty jealousies, turf battles, and the like."[6]

> ### There's no shortage of garden-variety human failings that sour people on the faith.

Some personalities are more susceptible to hurt than others. It's entirely possible for two people to grow up in the same church, and even the same family, and for one to be hurt, and for another to emerge with their faith relatively unscathed. What's important is the perception of abuse. If someone feels they've been victimized, and associates that hurt with God, it's more likely that they will experience struggles with their faith.

## HURT BY PEOPLE, DISAPPOINTED WITH GOD

There's another important distinction to make when thinking about recoilers. So far, I've been writing about those who are hurt by the people in their lives. They have become disillusioned with faith because the people they sanctified let them down. God is guilty by association.

However, not all recoilers fit this description. There are those who feel directly hurt or disappointed by God. They hold God responsible for experiences as disparate as extended spiritual dryness to misfortune in life.

In 1988 Christian author Philip Yancey wrote *Disappointment with God*. Despite the book's audacious title—or perhaps because of it—the book struck a chord and became a bestseller. In the book Yancey relays dozens of stories of disenchanted Christians, but perhaps the most disturbing was the story of Richard, a young seminary student Yancey mentored. One day Richard visited Yancey and made a shocking confession. "'I hate God!'" he blurted out. "'No, I don't mean that. I don't even believe in Him.'"

What had happened? In the months previous to his meeting with Yancey, Richard had suffered a string of misfortunes: his parents divorced, his fiancé left him, and a promising job opportunity fell through. One night after hours of seemingly fruitless prayer, Richard grabbed his Bible and gathered his Christian books and burned them on the barbeque outside his apartment. As the flames engulfed his books, he felt liberated. "'I felt converted—but converted *from* God.'"

Experiences like Richard's are disturbing. Unfortunately they are not rare. A 2004 study found that 50 percent of college students reported having negative feelings toward God when recalling disappointing events in which they believe God played a role. In another recent study, 21 percent of college students reported that their belief in God's existence decreased in the wake of a major negative life event that they attributed to God. Nine percent of students sampled in the study responded by declaring that God did not exist.

Citing the results of these studies, Exline writes: "In such cases, people can develop intense anger and mistrust toward God . . . some people might even decide to abandon belief altogether as a result of such incidents." The study also yielded another interesting find: "Further analyses identified a group of *conflicted unbelievers*, individuals who reported strong negative emotions toward God but were not certain whether to believe in God. These data corroborate clinical accounts of *emotional atheism*, in which people who feel wounded by God decide that God does not exist."[7]

Deciding that God does not exist seems to be a common response to disappointment with God. In Yancey's account of

Richard's dramatic deconversion, Richard first blurts out, "I hate God!" Only after he catches himself does he say, "No, I don't mean that. I don't even believe in Him." One can't help but wonder if his first utterance was the truer indication of his feelings. Often disbelief is only a smoke screen, a reflex of recoilers to mask deep disillusionment and pain.

# 6- Reaching Recoilers

Toward the end of my conversation with Katie, she exhibited a friendlier attitude toward Christianity. It wasn't because of anything I'd said. It was due to the compelling example of her youngest sister, Dana, a committed Christian.

Even though Dana was just nineteen years old, Katie looked up to her.

"She's my hero," Katie said. "An amazing human being."

What had so impressed Katie? For starters, Dana was selfless. She shaved her head to raise money for cancer research. For Christmas, she asked her family to forgo buying her presents and instead buy a cow for a family overseas.

"Here we were, listing all the presents we wanted," Katie recalled, "and she just wanted to help someone else."

Katie also praised Dana for her decision to attend Bible college. Only minutes earlier Katie had expressed doubt about God's very existence. Now she was downright giddy when describing her sister's missionary training.

"Dana went to China as part of her program. Isn't that incredible?" she said.

Katie didn't even mind when Dana talked about her faith. "She mentions God casually, but she doesn't preach at me," Katie said. "But when she talks about God, she really lights up. I think that's amazing. She's the kind of person who can talk to someone like me."

*She's the kind of person who can talk to someone like me.* As I listened to Katie, I wondered if Dana wasn't the reason Katie hadn't slammed the door on her faith altogether. Dana wasn't an expert, but she was on to something. How was she able to make such a profound impact on her jaded older sister? And how might we impact recoilers in a similar way?

## EMPATHY, NOT ARGUMENTS

In the last chapter, I cited studies showing that many young adults resolve anger toward God by deciding that He doesn't exist. This surprising but common reaction can result in confusion for Christians: Leavers may claim intellectual skepticism when, in reality, they left because they were hurt. A well-meaning Christian may engage their arguments but miss the underlying cause of their departure entirely.

How do we avoid making this mistake? We can start by doing a little detective work. Before responding to a leaver's stated objections, ask some questions about their experience within the faith: *Have you encountered Christians you consider hypocritical or cruel? How would you characterize your childhood experience with the faith?*

Often these types of questions will elicit stories that give you a window into the person's experience, and let them open up about their grievances. But be careful not to ask questions that put them on the defensive, or even questions that are too direct, such as "Have you been hurt by Christians?" or "Are you mad at God?" They may sidestep such inquiries, because they find them too personal to answer.

Once they begin sharing their stories, watch for certain signs. If they deride Christians with emotional fervor, that may suggest a damaging encounter. Listen too for questions that deal with the problem of suffering. Someone who asks, "If a loving God exists, why is there so much suffering in the world?" may really be asking, "Why didn't God intervene when I was hurt?"

Once you've established that the person fits the description of a recoiler, dispense with arguments. Concentrate on learning that person's story. When you hear how they were hurt, empathize with their pain. Psychologist Gunnoe says, "First, you have to send the message that you're there for that person emotionally. 'I will cry with you. I will curse with you.' Only later can you hope to talk through other things." Empathy—not arguments—is what they truly need at this point. Resist the impulse to quickly interpret their story or offer reasons for why they suffered. Christian clichés such as "It's all part of God's will" or "God lets things happen for a reason" can sound like insults to a person who has suffered deeply. Gunnoe cautions, "The fact that this bad thing happened for a reason—that's a conclusion they have to reach on their own. Being told too quickly that 'it's all God's will' could just make them angrier." Instead, Gunnoe advises, "You're much better off saying this is a horrible evil thing that happened to you, and I don't understand it either. I'm here and I'm angry for you."[1]

## THINKING BIBLICALLY ABOUT PAIN

Most recoilers are hurt by relationships, so it's unsurprising that their healing must come in the context of relationship. "Form a relationship," advises psychologist Edward Shafranske. "It's within the context of a relationship that healing will take place. That's where they can talk through and deal with the experiences they've had." Most often, only after establishing friendships with recoilers will you be able to speak into their lives in a meaningful way.

If you're fortunate enough to earn their trust, at some point it will be necessary to help them make sense of their hurtful experiences. "You will come to a point where you must offer the person a theologically satisfying explanation for what happened," says Gunnoe. "There has to be some instruction about how to read the Bible differently or reconcile their experiences within the Christian tradition."

Part of that instruction, Shafranske says, is delineating the line between God and the people who hurt them in His name. "Work with them on reconciliation. But help them make the distinction between reconciliation with the people who hurt them and reconciliation with God." And don't push too quickly for full reconciliation with their abusers. "It may take time for them to forgive," says Shafranske, "and they may never again join their old church or faith community."[2] The important thing at this point is that recoilers learn to make sense of their pain, and open themselves to the presence of a loving God.

**How do we expect them to want something that we don't appear to even enjoy?**

## ENJOY YOUR FAITH

Evangelist TV Thomas offered me a surprising bit of wisdom for reaching ex-Christians. "For goodness sakes, enjoy your faith!"

he bellowed in his distinctive Malaysian accent. "Christians get so tense and serious. They forget to show their friends and family that the Christian life is filled with joy."

Thomas makes an excellent point. I think too often when a friend or loved one strays from the faith we freeze in a defensive crouch and lose our joy. Our concern for their spiritual well-being actually causes us to adopt a dour demeanor. But how do we expect them to want something that we don't appear to even enjoy? Remember what impressed Katie about her sister, Dana? She noticed that Dana would "really light up" when she talked about God. This may sound too simple, but I wonder how much better all leavers would respond if they saw us "light up" when we talked about our faith.

We have rich truths to offer the recoilers in our lives. The Bible is a deep well for the abused and broken. And the God it reveals is not some distant deity, standing aloof from His creation. Instead He chose to delve into the mess of humanity, knowing it would break His heart. As a result we have a high priest who is "touched by our afflictions," a divine sufferer to accompany us in our darkest hours. To all who suffer we can point to His cross, a bold promise that even the worst injustices can ultimately lead to redemption.

# Portrait of a RECOILER

E ric's faith was in trouble even before "the accident." He gave his heart to Jesus as a ten-year-old, and attended Christian school. His biggest spiritual influence was his grandmother, a woman whom he describes as "the sweetest lady in the world" and a "Baptist to the core." During his teens Eric started to play hooky on Sunday mornings, but he never doubted his faith.

That all changed after high school when he became a police officer. The soul-numbing tragedies he witnessed on the job exacted a heavy toll.

"I know the religious arguments about why there's evil in the world," Eric said. "But encountering it in the real world is different."

His voice tightened as he recalled what he'd seen.

"You go to child rape scenes, multiple murder scenes, suicide scenes—the most grotesque movies don't hold a candle to what actually happens. You see firsthand just how brutal human beings can be to each other."

The evil started to corrode his belief in God. "You start questioning, if there is a good God, how can He possibly let such atrocities occur?"

It was as Eric wrestled with such questions, that the accident occurred. This time he not only witnessed tragedy; he played a part in it.

It happened during a training exercise. Eric and his fellow SWAT team members were practicing entry techniques on a mock building. They broke for lunch and hit the

SWAT transport van to reload their weapons. Eric was having difficulty loading a magazine into his rifle and grabbed another magazine from the drawer in the van, not knowing that the drawer was stocked with live ammunition for SWAT callouts.

When the training resumed, Eric fired his weapon with deadly consequences. He shot a fellow officer in the head and killed him. It wasn't just any officer. It was Eric's close friend. Eric was the one who recruited him into the force.

After the accident Eric turned in his badge, but his career wasn't the only thing that ended that day.

"That snapped that last thread of my faith," Eric said, remembering his deceased friend. "He was the kind of guy who would give you the shirt off his back. He had a wife and two kids. And there he was lying on the floor with his brains all over my lap. God works in mysterious ways? That just doesn't cut it."

After the accident, Eric found it easy to build a case against God.

"I started looking for all the hypocrisy in Christians," he said. "It seemed to me that the people that were shouting the loudest had the most skeletons in their closets."

Eric doesn't claim to have all the answers and admits to living a self-destructive life in a desperate attempt to block out the painful memories. "I drink, I do everything short of illegal drugs, and I take risks, anything to get a break from the images in my head."

Part of his attempt to flee the memories is to travel. "You name the place, I've probably been there. People think that's cool, but they don't know that it's me trying to escape. It's me running."

Eric's grandmother continues to pray for him, and he

hasn't completely shut the door on God. One of his recent trips took him to Israel. When he visited the River Jordan, he did something surprising.

"I baptized myself," he said. "I thought, why do I need a priest or a preacher to do this for me? So I absolved myself of all my sins, and I jumped into the river and completely submersed myself."

Why did he do it?

"I don't know," he said. "It was exciting. I mean, this is where Christ was baptized. And my goodness, if you're standing at the River Jordan, you should go in. I'm still searching, I guess."

# Section 3

## Modern Leavers

# 7 - Dawkins Disciples

J oin Us!"
My hand froze on my computer mouse, unable to
click the invitation. The cursor hovered over the button.

Did I really want to attend meetings of the Wheaton
Atheists Group?

I had already interviewed dozens of atheists, but most
of my interviews had been conducted over the phone or
via email. Somehow the prospect of sitting face-to-face
with them was more intimidating. I wasn't afraid of an
intellectual assault. Yes, there would be plenty of God-
bashing in these meetings, but I wasn't likely to hear anything new. Thanks to my peculiar habit of reading reams
of atheist literature, I'd heard most of the arguments
against Christianity before and all from the movement's
most eloquent spokespeople.

Rather it was the personal nature of these encounters that I found unsettling. These weren't disembodied
stories or abstract arguments. These were real people,
and they'd be venting disdain for the God I believe in and

love. Talking to them over the phone was one thing; sitting face-to-face, eating chicken wings together at a local restaurant would be different. Still I wanted to meet ex-Christians. And judging from the online comments from members, this group was a gold mine.

But why seek out *atheists*?

## DIGGING FOR WORLDVIEWS

Through my conversations with ex-Christians, I learned that they were a diverse group of people. Some leave for personal reasons, as we have seen. Others reject the faith out of a "true for you but not for me" mind-set. But, as I discovered, yet another group of young leavers has fled the faith for intellectual reasons. Unlike postmodern leavers, they love linear thinking, objective truth, and the Western tradition of rational thought. If anything, most of them feel Christian faith is *too* concerned for the marginalized, a dangerous naiveté in a Darwinian, survival-of-the-fittest world. I have identified these leavers as modernists in reference to the philosophical tradition that undergirds their beliefs. Interestingly, I found that many of these kinds of thinkers were also atheists. By seeking out ex-Christians at an atheist meeting, I hoped to gain greater insight into this second worldview. I wasn't disappointed.

## AN UNDERWORLD OF DOUBT

Frankly, I was surprised to learn that an atheist group even existed in my neighborhood. Wheaton, Illinois, is a Christian powerhouse, an "evangelical Vatican," as the *New York Times* has stated. Throw a stick and you'll hit a church—and probably a parachurch organization too. I work in the area at Christianity Today International, a magazine and online publisher that reaches a total of six million readers. The sprawling campus of Tyndale House—publisher of the bestselling Left Behind series—sits so close to our offices that staffers literally walk over advance copies of their new books. Just down the road loom the castle-like buildings of Wheaton College, known as the "Christian Harvard" and the alma mater of Billy Graham. There's no shortage of churches either. According to some estimates, Wheaton has the most churches per capita of any city in the world.[1]

 **These weren't people meeting merely for intellectual stimulation; they were huddling together for warmth.**

No wonder area skeptics felt outnumbered. "Looking to meet like-minded individuals in a nation that is cuckoo for Christianity!" wrote one atheist on the Meetup site. "In a suburb filled with people that seem to be extremely narrow-minded and faith-centric, it'll be nice to meet like-minded folks," wrote another. These weren't people meeting merely for intellectual stimulation; they were huddling together for warmth. The surrounding Christian culture was an ever-present challenge to their beliefs and a constant reminder of the faith many of them had left behind. Still, they had an impressive network of "free-thinkers." Just scanning their site opened my eyes to a whole underworld of doubt. There was a "Skeptics in the Park" group, a "Free Inquiry" club, even a "Latino Atheists Meetup."

When I finally worked up the courage to click the "Join Us!" button to receive meeting details, I was greeted by a picture of Greg, the group's organizer. I guessed Greg to be in his mid-thirties, not much older than me. He was dressed impeccably, but looked dangerously thin with a head that probably appeared larger than it really was thanks to his slight frame and receding hairline. He looked directly into the camera with serious, intelligent eyes that seemed to dance with doubt. I had to chuckle—he fit my mental image of an atheist to a T.

Judging from the online comments of the members, however, these meetings weren't somber, academic affairs. In fact, for most participants fun and community seemed to be the big draws. "Nogodformethanks" boasted on the message board, "We have a fun, friendly group!" They met at local pubs, or in homes. Some of the online pictures taken at their house meetings were indistinguishable from the church small group I attend every Wednesday.

## IN THE PRESENCE OF MY "ENEMIES"

The next meeting would be at a pub less than a mile from my house. I showed up feeling a little jittery. What was I—a Bible-believing Christian since my youth—going to say to atheists? How would they react when they learned that I was a Christian? Would it be all-out war? I intended to observe, ask questions, and then keep my mouth shut . . . but I'm not very good at keeping my mouth shut. And some of them would be expecting me. In my online profile I'd written that I was a "Christian journalist writing a book about ex-Christians."

When I walked into the pub, I didn't know where to find them.

"I'm looking for a group of people," I told the host.

His face was blank. Obviously there were many "groups of people" in the pub.

"They're, um, atheists," I offered.

Those were the magic words. He pointed me to three adjoined tables near the back of the bar where a large group had already assembled. I walked over and introduced myself to the young man opposite the table from me. He shook his head.

"I saw your profile. I know who you are." He let out a mock groan. "Why did I have to sit on *this* end of the table?"

Not exactly the reception I had hoped for.

Before I could respond, a gray-haired woman smiled warmly in my direction. "I don't think I've seen you here before. What's your name?"

"I'm Drew," I said cheerfully. "I work just across the street at Christianity Today."

Her brow furrowed. "When did you become an atheist?"

"I didn't. I'm a Christian."

The word "Christian" seemed to hang in the air. The conversations around the table died, and I felt twenty-five pairs of eyes fasten upon me.

## ATHEISM AMPLIFIED

I had told several friends and family members of my plans to attend the meeting. Some of them weren't sure about the idea. My wife, Grace, was particularly worried. She knew all too well my argumentative nature and was worried about how atheists might react to my presence. Suddenly I was wondering if she had been right. I thought they'd be grateful for the chance to discuss their beliefs with a Christian. Instead they seemed irritated, even hostile.

Maybe I shouldn't have been surprised by their reaction. Emboldened by a newfound public prominence, many atheists have grown more combative as of late. Atheists used to cluster in academic coteries. Today they're mainstream and pushing for more influence in the public square. They plaster anti-God messages on billboards and buses, deride Christians as "Faith heads" while their most prominent proponents call for outlandish legislation, such as forbidding parents to teach religious ideas to their own children.[2]

Perhaps their greatest victories have come in the publishing arena. There was a time when atheist literature was confined to cumbersome college textbooks and dusty classics by David Hume, Friedrich Nietzsche, and Bertrand Russell. How times have changed! Visit your local bookstore and you'll encounter a raft of new books from atheist authors. And unlike the skeptics of the past who couched their denials of the divine in tangled academic prose, these new skeptics are popularizers—writers with a gift for communicating with a wide audience.

The authors at the center of this publishing storm have been dubbed the "new atheists." Their books bear provocative titles such as *God Is Not Great*, *The God Delusion*, and *The End of Faith*. During the past few years these books have rocketed to the top of the *New York Times* bestseller list and gained widespread media attention.

The "new atheists" title is not completely deserved; there's really nothing new about what these atheists are writing. They specialize in dredging up old arguments against God's existence and peddling them to a credulous public. What's new is the attitude. They're confrontational, angry, and militant. The movement's de facto leader, Richard Dawkins (*The God Delusion*), is on a crusade to stamp out religious belief by making it "too embarrassing" to believe in God. Dawkins is an aggressive proselytizer and savvy businessman, selling not only millions of books but all manner of paraphernalia on his site, including tote bags, coffee mugs, T-shirts, stickers, and buttons. His website also has a "conversion corner," or more accurately put, a *de*conversion corner, where acolytes write their accounts of leaving Christianity. When I checked it there were 679 "Testimonies" and counting.

Christopher Hitchens, another prominent atheist author (*God Is Not Great*) spares no believer in his assault on religion. Even Mother Teresa comes under his fire, as he graphically proclaims his desire for the late humanitarian to go to a place he himself does not believe in. Perhaps it was this kind of vitriol that prompted pastor and apologist Douglas Wilson to say that the new atheists really have two tenets. "One: there is no God. Two: I hate Him."

The new atheists' incendiary language has simultaneously repelled some and attracted others, while providing the impetus for atheists to confront religious adherents whom they regard as backward and benighted.

## "I ALWAYS BELIEVED THE EARTH WAS 6,000 YEARS OLD"

As I sat at the table, questions started coming from every direction.

"Why did you come? Why are you writing this book? How can you believe in God?"

I tried to keep my answers short. I didn't want to monopolize the conversation. After all, I was there to observe. I wanted to listen to them. But as the night wore on, I found myself embroiled in passionate but courteous debate. Some around the table seemed to warm to me, especially as I commended them for their intellectual curiosity and demonstrated a familiarity with their favorite atheist authors.

Somewhere in the midst of our conversations, a jovial young man named Dan came clean as a former Christian. He'd left the faith only months earlier.

"I was in the Assemblies of God all my life," he said. "I even played in a Christian band."

What had caused his crisis of faith?

"I always believed the earth was 6,000 years old," Dan said bitterly. "But now I know it's not."

For years Dan tried desperately to maintain his belief in the young earth theory. He read material from Answers in Genesis, a Christian apologetics organization, consulted his pastor and people in his church. But ultimately he said he just couldn't deny what he saw as the evidence that the world was much older than 6,000 years.

"That's when I realized that Christianity just wasn't true," he said.

Inwardly I cringed at the false-alternatives scenario that Dan had set up in his mind. For him, one geological question (which the Bible doesn't even address explicitly) was the deciding factor for faith. Even Answers in Genesis, which holds unswervingly to a literal reading of the Bible's first book, seems to place less importance on the earth's age. The first bullet point of their statement of belief reads: "The scientific aspects of creation are important, but are secondary in importance to the proclamation of the Gospel of Jesus Christ as Sovereign, Creator, Redeemer and Judge."[3] However, for Dan, the question of the earth's age was paramount, and in his view Christianity had failed.

I had some good conversations with Dan and the other atheists around the table. But I could sense that my presence was disruptive to the regular flow of the meeting. And ultimately, it wasn't welcomed. Halfway through the evening, I was gently but firmly disinvited to future gatherings. They had come to the meeting anticipating a relaxing night of making fun of televangelists and passing around creationist tracts. Having to defend their beliefs against someone from the other side probably wasn't what they had in mind on that Thursday evening. But the night was not a total loss. I'd met some new friends with whom I promised to stay in touch, and I gained valuable insight into the mind-set of a new kind of leaver.

# Theological QUIBBLES

I realize that labeling people as "ex-Christians" invites controversy. Can someone who truly received Christ ever fall away? Were such people even saved in the first place?

Many would say "no." God predestines His children and secures their eternal destiny. Any talk of leaving God's family is nonsense. Those who claim to walk away are mistaken: they were never Christians in the first place.

Just as strident are those who claim that true deconversion is possible. They cite their own biblical passages that seem to suggest that straying from the fold is all-too-real a danger.

My purpose here is not to join the debate. I don't use terms such as "leavers" or "ex-Christians" to assert that the leavers I interviewed were ever Christians in any ultimate sense. And I'm not saying that they weren't. The truth is, I don't know. Ultimately, only God does. I use terms like "ex-Christians" to honor how the people I interviewed saw themselves. They believed that they were once members of the Christian family. To say that they weren't would mean speaking over their voices. I thought it was important to respect the way they describe themselves in order to have the kind of conversations that will open their hearts to God—an objective we can all agree is worth pursuing.

## MEDIUM AND MESSAGE

Salvation isn't the only hot potato here. I identify categories of leavers for a specific purpose: to help us think about how we can adapt our approach to reach each kind. I argue that we should approach postmodern leavers differently than we do modern leavers. Recoilers require an entirely different approach, as do neo-pagans, and so on. We change the way we share the gospel to match our listener's needs. In order to effectively call them back, we must understand why they left. The factors that lead them away often act as barriers that prevent their return.

Some Christians will cry foul. They object to tailoring the gospel message to appeal to different audiences. Just tell it like it is, they say. Give everyone the same message and leave the results up to God. Changing methods is tantamount to selling out the gospel. For them, the medium is the message.

I disagree. In Scripture, the message was often tailored for its audience. Jesus never approached two people the same way. He spoke differently to Pharisees than He did to the woman caught in adultery. He approached the woman at the well one way, and the rich young ruler another. He never changed the essence of His message, but His approach was as different as His listeners.

Paul continued this trend with his commitment to "become all things to all men." At Mars Hill he used the idolatrous practices of pagan philosophers as his sermon opener, and then proceeded to quote a Greek poet to describe humanity's connection to God. Paul was a master chameleon, dedicated to spreading the trans-ethnic, transcultural message of the gospel. He didn't require that people cross cultures to come to God, and neither must we. In a pluralistic society, these examples are more important than ever to follow. The gospel never changes, but the way we share it does.

# 8 - Modern Man

When I encountered Rich, I didn't have to broach the topic of faith. He brought it up the first time we met, taking no pains to mask his antipathy.

"How can you believe in religion? If the Bible is true why are there no miracles today?"

With Abe, I'd been caught off guard. This time I recognized the worldview. So I saved my new friend some breath.

"Let me guess," I responded. "You believe that everything we don't understand we automatically consign to the realm of the supernatural—a tendency that only demonstrates our ignorance and fear of the unknown. Science will eventually eliminate the need for religion by pushing back the boundaries of knowledge, elucidating all mysteries."

He was a little stunned to hear this coming from a Christian. "Yeah . . . that's about it," he agreed.

Rich was a modernist.

I encountered Rich years ago, but as I sat in the Wheaton atheist meeting I was experiencing a strong sense of déjà vu. The worldview to which Rich subscribed was very much alive. At the atheist meeting, my new Pentecostal-turned-atheist friend, Dan, hit me with virtually the same question Rich had posed years earlier.

"If God is real, where are the miracles?"

## BREAKING IT DOWN

What is modernism?

Since postmodern thinking developed as a reaction to modernism, it is no surprise that the two are very different. From a modernist perspective, "There is no such thing as a spirit, soul or the supernatural," writes apologist Rick Wade. Modernists believe that truth isn't found through revelation but through scientific investigation and reason. The twentieth-century thinkers who promoted modernism argued that "knowledge now had to be dispassionate, objective, and certain."[1] In this worldview, there is simply no room for belief in anything outside the physical world.

To understand how modernism developed, we have to take a quick trip back to the seventeenth century. Many historians trace the origins of modern thought to the French philosopher and mathematician Rene Descartes. On one fateful day, while in Germany, Descartes was forced indoors by bad weather. He sat alone in a stove-heated room gazing out the window at the city's architecture. He observed that many of the city's buildings were crumbling. Some could be fixed with minor repair, he speculated. But for those buildings with bad foundations, there could be no such remedy. If the foundations were poor, the buildings were doomed. The only solution for such buildings, Descartes mused, was to tear them down and build from scratch.

Then the proverbial light bulb went on. Descartes realized that buildings weren't so different from systems of belief. Shaky foundations spelled trouble for both. If a "building" of belief had a weak foundation, patchwork repairs would not suffice. No belief could be true if it rested on flawed assumptions about the nature of reality. To create a truly secure structure of beliefs, one would need to tear down the existing structure, establish a firm foundation, and build again.

That's just what Descartes set out to do with his own beliefs. He questioned everything he'd ever been taught and tested new beliefs rigorously, ensuring they were strong enough to support each new conviction. Using this method he endeavored to rebuild the superstructure of his beliefs, brick by logical brick.

But where could he begin? He needed an "indubitable" foundation upon which to build, something he could know with absolute certainty. But what could serve as that rock solid base? Descartes dismissed divine revelation as an appropriate foundation. It was delivered to humans, and humans were fallible. Even physical reality was not beyond doubt. After all, it took human senses to apprehend the physical world. And human senses were susceptible to deception. In fact the unreliability of human perception seemed to plague even the most basic beliefs.

Ultimately Descartes found his foundation, not in the exterior world, but in the interiority of his own mind. The one thing that was beyond doubt, he decided, was the fact that he was thinking. Even if he began to doubt whether he was truly thinking, he couldn't doubt it for long. Why? Because the very ability to entertain doubt required thought! There was no way around it—the fact that he was thinking was indubitable. And this ability to think was proof positive that he existed. He verbalized this idea in the now-famous maxim: "*Cogito Ergo Sum.*" Translated into English it reads, "I think, therefore I am."

Descartes' approach to discovering truth had a profound impact on the Western world. First, his knowledge-as-a-building-metaphor changed the way we talked about how and what we believe. How often do we say an argument must be "supported" or rest on a secure "foundation"? How often do we dismiss fallacious arguments as "baseless" or "weak"? Whenever we use such language, we pay homage to the founding father of modernism.

Descartes' ideas had another crucial impact. Since time immemorial, authorities were the arbiters of truth. If you had a question about God you consulted a priest or comparable spiritual leader. If you sought wisdom you might ask the village elders. But the advent of modernism turned this conventional thinking on its head. Reason—and not authority—was deemed the best source of guidance about truth, morality, and even God. No truth claim, no matter how venerated its speaker, was considered credible unless it could be verified through reason.

> **The Bible held that "the fear of the Lord" was the beginning of wisdom. Not so for modernists.**

Descartes was a devout Catholic whose whole philosophical project was motivated by a desire to prove the credibility of the faith. Yet his legacy was quickly co-opted by people with different agendas. Descartes' method of investigating reality became one of the main weapons in the arsenal of those Enlightenment thinkers who aimed to discredit Christian faith. Most importantly, Descartes had unwittingly removed revelation as the primary basis for knowledge. The Bible held that the "fear of the Lord" was the beginning of wisdom. Not so for modernists. Descartes created a system of thought that required no appeal to divine truth; it rested completely on human understanding. Today modernism is strongly associated with naturalism or empiricism, worldviews that negate the supernatural and accept only truth claims that are readily apprehended with the five senses or grasped with reason.

## CLASH OF WORLDVIEWS

"Where are the miracles?"

The question seemed to linger on Dan's lips. His already angular face seemed to harden even more.

His follow-up question too exposed a deep suspicion of supernatural claims. "Jesus said you could tell mountains to jump into the ocean," he said. "That doesn't work!"

Dan leaned across the table. His hands shot into the air in a mock petition toward heaven.

I knew I had to be careful with my response. Should I recount the dozens of miracle stories I'd heard from missionaries abroad? I could even share personal answers to prayer or things that I'd witnessed that could only be described as supernatural. But I held my tongue. I knew such stories would get me nowhere. The missionary miracles would meet with extreme skepticism and likely mockery. The atheists would pounce on the fact that the miracles in question occurred in poor nations among uneducated people. They would argue that such people are awash in superstition and easy marks for emotional suggestibility. My own stories might fare slightly better, but ultimately they would be deemed too subjective as well. In fact, I received the distinct impression that anything short of producing a miracle or display of magic in that place, at that very moment, would be unsatisfactory. Besides, there were other dynamics at play. There was a yawning chasm between our worldviews, and that needed to be addressed first.

The middle-aged Englishman to my right seemed like the

most sophisticated thinker in the group. Other members of the group deferred to him. His training was in physics, and I ribbed him playfully about recent advances in the field that seemed to point to a creator.

"For hundreds of years the universe was thought to be infinite with no beginning or end," I said. "But since Einstein we know that it had a definite beginning. Doesn't that smack of creation to you?"

He smiled wryly. "Yes, but the church got along perfectly well for hundreds of years without that scientific knowledge."

That exchange led to an interesting conversation about a variety of topics. We discussed physics, where his expertise clearly outmatched mine. Then we talked about the life of Jesus and the history of Christianity, where the tables turned in my favor.

My conversation partner even came to my defense when another atheist claimed that "you don't need philosophy" to debate God's existence. I insisted that the debate over God's existence necessarily entailed a discussion of philosophy, and pointed out that his statement that reality can only be discovered with the five senses betrayed a working philosophy called empiricism.

"He's right," my English friend said reluctantly. "All beliefs have underlying philosophies."

That gave me a chance to delineate our differing worldviews.

"I don't blame you for rejecting any claims of the supernatural," I said. "In fact, I'd be surprised if you didn't."

Eyebrows raised around the table.

"Then why do *you* believe in the supernatural?" someone asked.

"From what I've heard here, most of you are naturalists, meaning that you deny reality beyond the physical world. Is that right?"

Several of them nodded yes.

"So if naturalism is the lens through which you view life, then any supernatural claims are rejected a priori. Your worldview simply doesn't have room for such claims."

Again they had to agree. One even admitted that he'd encountered phenomena that he couldn't explain, but that it didn't trouble him. "I just shrug and move on," he said.

# 9 - Speaking to Modern Leavers

If you were to die tonight, would you go to heaven?"
This popular question originally appeared in a program called Evangelism Explosion, created by the late evangelist and megachurch pastor D. James Kennedy. The query quickly became a favorite among evangelists. To this day it's often used as an icebreaker for spiritual conversations with unbelievers—and why not? What better way to focus a conversation on the all-important question of eternity?

But there can be a problem with this kind of question. It assumes your listener already shares some key Christian beliefs: a belief in the afterlife (in heaven specifically) and by extension, a belief in God. That's a lot to assume!

I remember watching a Christian program on which evangelists posed a similar question to strangers on the street. One young man they approached shook his head when he heard the question.

"Man, I don't even believe in all that stuff."

The evangelist seemed stumped. He backed up, repeated his charge that the man was a sinner, and asked the question again.

Here too the evangelist made the mistake of assuming too much common ground. Such an approach may work well in a Christian culture, where the majority of people hold to a Christian worldview. However, in our increasingly secular culture, it simply won't suffice, no matter how consistently or forcefully such questions are posed. When you talk across disparate worldviews, your words disappear in the void.

This kind of approach, when used in a debate, is actually a formal fallacy. Philosophers call this "begging the question," using the premises of your opinion to try to prove that your opinion is valid. Do angels exist? Of course they do—they can fly! That's begging the question. So is assuming that people who have left the faith still hold core Christian beliefs.

Yet this is what so many Christians do with family members and friends who have left the faith. They continue talking to them as if they still believe. Recently I was told of a Christian couple whose grown daughter had left the faith. The parents tried to persuade the daughter to return, using arguments from Scripture.

**When you talk across disparate worldviews, your words disappear in the void.**

This only further alienated the daughter, who made it clear she no longer regarded the Bible as authoritative. The parents apparently failed to learn much from this first exchange. The mother's latest attempt to win her daughter back was to write a heavy-handed letter listing biblical passages that condemned her daughter's lifestyle. The daughter had rejected the Bible as God's Word; citing chapter and verse was futile. Yet somehow the mother thought that if she just clobbered her daughter with enough biblical truth, she'd come back.

## QUESTIONING—AND VALIDATING

Assuming common beliefs may not work, but it's definitely more comfortable. By keeping the discussion on your turf, you can avoid doing the hard work of addressing underlying worldviews. But talking about worldviews is exactly what's needed. This is crucial when talking to modern leavers who are particularly sensitive to logical leaps. They rightly tune us out when we make arguments based upon premises that they do not share.

Instead, ask questions designed to unearth their worldviews. *How do you determine what's true? Do you consider yourself spiritual? Who do you really admire?* Asking these kinds of questions will accomplish at least a few objectives. First, it will make leavers feel validated and grateful that a Christian has actually given them an opportunity to describe what they believe. "Being listened to" is powerful, and it will make them more open to listen to what you have to say. Second, you will actually understand what leavers believe, and more importantly, how they came to hold those beliefs. This will allow you to tailor your presentation of the gospel to specifically address their concerns. It will also level the ground as you discuss your beliefs. If you fail to unearth worldviews, conversations about God can devolve into a trial of Christian faith. Suddenly it seems like you're the only one who has beliefs to defend. In reality everyone, whether Christian or not, has a whole set of beliefs that require defending. Once both worldviews are out in the open, it means they too must defend their worldviews.

When I had dinner with the area atheists, they shot questions rapid-fire, trying to undermine my beliefs. It was quickly turning into a sort of kangaroo court in which my Christian beliefs were on trial. The moment I identified their worldview, we were able to deal with their beliefs and discover the true obstacles to faith.

"I could give you the best proofs for God's existence or

compelling evidences for the resurrection of Christ," I told them. "But until you're willing to soften your worldview and at least consider the possibility of the supernatural, my arguments will fall on deaf ears."

## DON'T FIGHT "PROXY WARS"

When the topic of faith gets too contentious, debate often gets channeled to other arenas. Rather than talk about God, you end up fighting "proxy wars" over inessentials. Yes, it's tempting to vent irritation over a leaver's party lifestyle, or political views, or immoral relationships, but none of these are your hill to die on. Save your most impassioned words to convey the life-giving power of the gospel.

**Your job isn't to straighten out all their opinions; it's to light the path back to Christ.**

Again, this is an especially important caveat when dealing with a modernist leaver. In my experience modernist leavers are the kind of people who love to debate. Perhaps this is no surprise given the high priority they place on logic and reason. This personality feature isn't confined to their views about God. These kinds of people often hold strong opinions on a variety of topics, and they're eager to defend them. That's why it's especially crucial to avoid getting sucked into debates about peripheral issues. Even if you manage to convince them that, say, your morality and politics are superior, will that really lead them back to the faith? Or is it more likely that you will win a pyrrhic victory that only further isolates them? Some of their opinions may well be contrary to Christian truth. But your job isn't to straighten out all their opinions; it's to light the path back to Christ, and let Him resume His transformational work in their lives.

The same principle applies to second-tier theological issues. Infant baptism versus believer's baptism, Calvinism versus Arminianism, women in ministry—most Christians have strong opinions on these and other important subjects. And discussion of these issues between believers is entirely appropriate. But when talking to leavers, steer away from these contentious topics. You don't want to litter the path with any extra obstacles to faith. Why should they be forced to buy into your particular brand of Christianity in order to rejoin God's family? We all have our pet theologies, but this is no time to champion them. Instead stick to the theological center, what Lewis termed "mere Christianity," those essentials of the faith on which orthodox Christians agree. Talk about Jesus—His life, death, and resurrection. Once a leaver becomes your brother or sister in Christ, you'll have plenty of opportunities to debate the finer points of Christian doctrine.

## WHAT'S THE ALTERNATIVE?

In *The Jesus I Never Knew*, Philip Yancey writes that one of the main reasons he's a Christian is "for lack of better options." Yancey's tongue-in-cheek confession touches on an important point. When someone rejects Christianity, it's valid to ask them to consider if the alternative is more satisfying.

When it comes to the modernist worldview, the answer has to be "no." Atheists may dress it up talking about enjoying the short span of a natural life, or claim there's something noble about staring unflinchingly into the abyss of oblivion, but after you peel away such rhetoric, it's a hopeless worldview.

Recently I read a sad news story on CNN.com about a young

actor who committed suicide. The reader comments below the story lamented the dangers of depression. But one reader, with a decidedly modern worldview, had a different take. "Truthteller" wrote:

> Why all the assumptions that he was depressed? Perhaps he was intelligent enough to deduce that life is meaningless. We are just another animal on the planet. When we die we cease to exist, just as we did not exist prior to birth. In 5 billion years the sun will consume the earth and the entire record of our species will be incinerated. It is obvious to the rational that there is either no god or there is a god and he is evil and takes delight in human suffering. Either way, this existence is a horrible nightmare, so it is completely understandable that one would choose to opt out. . . . Pleasure is the only rational reason for existence, so when pleasure is no longer possible the rational choice is death. When the pleasure goes out of my life, whether it be caused by old age or physical infirmity, I too will exercise my most basic fundamental human right: the right to end a miserable existence. Ultimately, we all will soon cease to exist and all of this will have meant nothing.

What was chilling to me about this comment (besides the fact that he seemed so hopeless) was that, based on an atheistic worldview, the reasoning was sound. Who could disagree with the commenter's conclusion if you accepted his premise that our entire species is bound for oblivion?

When we talk to modern leavers, we need to challenge them to ask themselves what they've really left for. To get an understanding of atheistic morality I talked to Greg Epstein, Harvard's "Humanist Chaplain" and author of the bestselling book *Good Without God*. My first question came right to the point.

"I understand that people can be good without God," I said. "My question is different. *Why should* people be good without God? What's the basis for your morality?"

Surprisingly he turned to the Golden Rule and rightly pointed out that if we failed to treat each other kindly, we'd ultimately bring destruction back on ourselves.

I agreed. But I wasn't satisfied with his answer.

"Philosophers might call that utilitarianism or acting based on 'enlightened self-interest,'" I said. "In other words, you're just being good so bad things don't happen to you. But is there no deeper reason to be good?"

"Well, I'm not a philosopher," he responded. "I'm not interested in finding some grand reason for morality."

Not only is this godless worldview ultimately hopeless, it's morally vacuous too. Dig down two inches and you strike air.

## TRUTH EXISTS—BUT WHOSE?

Some might assume that Christianity and modernism are implacable enemies. One seeks empirical proof, dismissing as superstitious any belief in the supernatural. The other focuses on the unseen, claiming that the physical world is but a shadow of a higher reality. The philosophical sparring of atheists and Christians fills our bookstores. (Remember, atheists are almost always modernists, since they absolutely negate God's existence.) But rarely do the entrenched debaters pause to consider how much they have in common. Actually the vitality of such debates testifies to the presence of some surprising common ground. On at least one crucial point, both modernists and Christians agree: truth and absolutes do exist, and they are worth fighting for!

So once you've shed light on their worldviews and beliefs, you can engage in traditional apologetics with modernist leavers.

These aren't people who are shy about truth claims. They just have different truth claims. So lay yours out with conviction.

Much has been made in recent years about how the postmodern wave has swept away the need for traditional apologetics. Popular Christian writer Donald Miller captured this sentiment perfectly in his bestselling memoir *Blue Like Jazz*: "The argument (over God's existence) stopped being about God a long time ago, and now it's about who is smarter, and honestly, I don't care. I don't believe I will ever walk away from God for intellectual reasons. Who knows anything anyway?[1]

For Miller, and many of his readers, the debate over God's existence or over any other similarly fraught doctrines may be irrelevant and boring. But this is not true of everyone, even of the younger generation. According to Lee Strobel, the largest group of readers who have come to Christ reading his book, *The Case for Christ*, has been sixteen- to twenty-four-year-olds.[2] In the last section I noted that postmodern leavers are practically allergic to traditional apologetics. But there are still plenty of modernist thinkers out there with whom Miller's glib dismissal of intellectual reasoning does not resonate.

> **"When we fail to give people good answers to their questions, we become another reason for them to disbelieve."**

Author and evangelist Mark Mittelberg believes that the rumors of modernity's death have been greatly exaggerated.

"I don't buy into the idea that people don't believe in logic anymore," says Mittelberg. "Even those who claim they don't believe in logic will give you logical reasons for not believing in it! Logic and evidence are inescapable tools."

Mittelberg recalls a quote he heard years ago from apologist Walter Martin that he says still haunts him: "When we fail to give people good answers to their questions, we become another reason for them to disbelieve."

According to Mittelberg, many young adults have been turned off by people with poor answers to their most vexing questions.

"A lot of young people look at their parents and say, 'You don't know why you believe this stuff. You don't have any answers.'"

One study on deconversion found that "the most frequently mentioned role of Christians in deconversion was in amplifying existing doubt." How did Christians manage to "amplify existing doubt"? The study found that deconverts reported "sharing their burgeoning doubts with a Christian friend or family member only to receive trite, unhelpful answers." The outcome was predictable. "These answers, in turn, moved them further away from Christianity."[3]

Mittelberg concedes that we can't always have all the answers, but he believes it's important to do our homework and give the best answers possible. "We don't always have to have answers at our fingertips. Even if we have to stop and say, 'That's a tough question. I'm going to spend a few weeks studying it and get back to you.' Not only will we give them a good answer to their question, we model a concern for truth."

*Model a concern for the truth*—excellent advice, especially when dealing with modernists for whom questions of truth figure so prominently.

As you launch into apologetics, there's another dynamic to keep in mind. Don't assume that leavers know the Bible or understand the Christian faith. After interviewing scores of ex-Christians, I've gotten used to biting my tongue when I hear patently false claims about Christianity. My patience, however, was really tested when I interviewed one young woman who intoned ominously about how "everyone thinks Jesus was a great guy, but most don't know He endorsed slavery." Jesus endorsing slavery? That was a new one to me. Among leavers, bizarre misperceptions of Christianity abound. It is crucial that Christians clearly communicate what the Bible says because many leavers simply do not know.

**Among leavers, bizarre misperceptions of Christianity abound.**

Also, don't assume that, even for modernists, apologetics alone can bring them back into the fold. Author and apologist Dinesh D'Souza describes apologetics as "mostly janitorial." That is, its purpose is to clear the path to God by removing obstacles to faith. Of course, that's an important function, but it isn't everything. As D'Souza writes, "ultimately it's God's love that has to work its way into a heart."

# Profile of a MODERNIST

S hane is twenty-six years old, married, and has three young boys. His cherubic features are offset by serious, close-set eyes and a well-trimmed beard. He speaks slowly and deliberately, as if testifying in court.

"I'm an atheist and an empiricist," he says. "I don't believe religion or psychics or astrology or anything supernatural. I'm a skeptic. I'm willing to be persuaded of different beliefs, but I would say, 'show me the evidence.'"

Raised in the Christian Reformed Church, Shane described his childhood experience with the faith as positive but insular. "I knew there were non-Christians, but I didn't know any. The church was our entire life."

When Shane was a teen, his dad had an affair with a younger woman and left the family. Shane was angry with his dad and at the church, which he says sided with his father. "That put me off organized religion," Shane said. "But I still believed in Jesus."

The next fall, when Shane started college, it was his first taste of the non-Christian world. "I finally met people outside my little bubble. I talked to people about their beliefs."

As he exchanged ideas with others, he started to doubt some of his beliefs. "I started doubting the whole idea of hell. How could God say that if you didn't do this one little thing—confess Jesus as Savior—that you're going to hell? All of the good stuff you do doesn't matter. If you don't say the right prayer you're going to a place with fire and poky things."

A complete loss of faith came gradually, but it was a process that he traces back to those initial misgivings. "I had little doubts that would nag at me," he says.

Then came what Shane calls "the straw that broke the camel's back": the terrorist attacks of September 11.

"Here was this group of people (terrorists) that believed God absolutely wanted them to do this. Yes, it wasn't my God. But how could I say that they were wrong, when my faith was based on as little evidence as theirs?"

Shane was also disgusted by how fellow Americans reacted to the terrorist attacks.

"There was this huge call back to religion. Everyone was talking about how God was on our side. I watched in horror. I started thinking that we've got it exactly backwards. We need less religion, not more. People started saying, 'We need God more than ever.'"

Shane disagreed: "No, we need reason more than ever! We need to calm down, stop worrying about what these ancient books say and figure out what to do."

Shane wasn't the only one similarly affected by September 11. The tragedy became a catalyst for many other atheists and the religiously ambivalent.

"I've heard this from people in the atheist community, over and over again. September 11 made us all realize that you can't be a fence-sitter on this issue. We realized that religion is causing these problems. It's holding belief in things which are not empirically verifiable. That's what's wrong."

Shane isn't categorically negative about his Christian past. He's grateful for his Christian education, which he says, "taught me how to think critically." He also says he misses the singing in church. "I especially loved the song

'Amazing Grace,'" he says, though he doesn't care for the lyrics. "What a horrible message! That we're all depraved wretches in need of a man in the sky to rescue us."

He's similarly critical of Jesus, though he's unsure if He even existed.

"The guy had a terrible temper. He could do some very nasty things to you, especially if you were a pig. He kills a fig tree. He's kind of a jerk. Not exactly the kind of person you would want to hang out with."

Shane admits that Jesus had some good things to say.

"The Golden Rule is great, but it's really a humanist notion."

Shane refers to himself repeatedly as a "professor." However when pressed, he admits he has no academic credentials and teaches only one introductory class at the local community college. His bigger platform is through a weekly podcast he does with two friends. And though the podcast's name has "doubt" in the title, Shane insists he's not out to persuade people of his beliefs.

"We just want to promote critical thinking," he says. "It's not like we're handing out pamphlets on the street. We're not trying to convert anyone."

When asked why he feels compelled to seek out a public forum to discuss his ideas, he chuckles. "A lot of us former Christians were vocal about our faith. Now we like to talk about our atheism. I guess it's the preacher gene."

# Section 4

## Neo-Pagans

# 10 - Wicca's Spell

I'm going to a Wiccan maypole dance!"
That was the answer I received from my neighbor when I inquired about her colorful, tasseled dress. Suddenly, I wished I hadn't asked. I didn't know much about Wicca, except that it made me very uncomfortable.

"Well, that's a very cool dress," was all I could manage in reply.

My wife and I had been friends with Lisa for months. She was eager to talk about spirituality. It was just a very different kind of spirituality than our own. We talked about Jesus. She spoke of her psychic abilities. We attended church. She participated in pagan rituals.

Lisa had grown up in the church, was active in her youth group, and still held some Christian beliefs, but was wary of the church. She did not consider herself a Wiccan per se. She was a dabbler. Like many other twenty-somethings, she had a fascination with alternative spiritualities. She loved tagging along with her Wiccan friends, and occasionally participating in their rituals.

## WICCA'S WOW

What exactly is Wicca?

It turns out that I wasn't alone in my ignorance—not a lot of Americans know. A 2009 Barna study found that 55 percent of Americans have not even heard of the term. But Wicca won't stay in the shadows for long. It's growing at a staggering rate. The number of Wiccans in the Unites States doubles approximately every thirty months, making it the nation's—and quite possibly the world's—fastest-growing religion. By 2012 some believe it could be the third largest religion in the United States.[1] According to polls conducted by the Covenant of the Goddess, the largest group of Wiccans in the United States, there are approximately eight hundred thousand Wiccans and other pagans in America.

However, since Wicca lacks any large-scale organizational structure, getting reliable statistics on the number of Wiccans is difficult. Complicating matters is the social stigma associated with witchcraft, an underlying practice of Wiccans. Since many may naturally feel reluctant about admitting to witchcraft, the actual number of Wiccans in the United States could be much higher. Some speculate it could be as high as three million. One thing beyond question is its popularity among young people. Harvard University lists more than one hundred Wiccan and pagan groups on college campuses nationwide.[2] As part of its New Religion in America special, "Teens and Wicca," National Public Radio called Wicca "one of the fastest-growing religions among high school and college students."[3]

Wicca, derived from the word *witchcraft*, is a neo-pagan, earth-based religion. Wiccans worship a goddess and a god, practice magic, worship nature, and engage in seasonal rituals. They believe in a unifying energy present in nature that can be manipulated through magic to bring personal rewards such as love, financial blessing, and general happiness. Though Wiccans worship gods, their conception of the divine is radically different from the Christian understanding. They deny a transcendent deity; the goddess and god are merely manifestations of nature's energy. Furthermore, Wiccans regard themselves as divine, and freely refer to themselves as gods or goddesses as well. One common Christian misperception is that Wiccans claim to worship the devil. Wiccans have no belief in the Christian God, or the biblical Satan.

Beyond these characteristics, it's a difficult religion to define. Wicca is a "religion of ritual," not theology, and as mentioned above, it has no centralized authority. Covens of witches add and subtract beliefs and practices at will. Due to the powerful role the Internet has played in the spread of Wicca, thousands now self-initiate, casting spells and performing rituals in the privacy of their homes.

Though many Wiccans claim that their religion possesses ancient roots, scholars agree that Wicca is actually a modern phenomenon, containing few if any ties to ancient paganism. It was founded in the mid–twentieth century by a retired British civil servant and occultist named Gerald Gardner, becoming "the only religion that England has given to the world," according to historian Michael Howard.[4] Though it originated in the United Kingdom, it quickly spread to other English-speaking countries. By the sixties and seventies, covens started springing up in the United States. Today there are Wiccans virtually everywhere on earth.

## FUELING THE MAGICAL FIRE

Though Wicca defines itself in opposition to mainstream culture, it benefits enormously from many popular trends. The first is feminism. Wicca's focus on a female deity makes it a magnet for those dissatisfied with patriarchal religion. Feminists flock to Wicca impressed by the feminine language and imagery that figure so prominently in its rituals. It's no surprise that more than two-thirds of Wiccans are female.

Consumerism also dovetails nicely with the burgeoning religion. Catherine Sanders, author of *Wicca's Charm*, writes, "Wicca benefits from our consumer-oriented society. It can be molded and shaped to fit the spiritual consumer's desire for experience. Instead of accepting a revealed truth, Wiccan seekers create their own truth and reality." Sanders writes, "Personal power is unlimited—Wiccans believe that their power is not limited by a deity, as in Christianity." Instead of glorifying a transcendent God, Wicca places the focus on adherents who are encouraged to use magical spells to fulfill their desires. Practitioners are free to pick and choose which beliefs and practices to adopt, making Wicca a religion tailor-made for our consumerist age.

However, nothing has benefited Wicca more than the environmental movement. Wiccans literally worship the earth, so their commitment to the environment is beyond question. For thousands seeking a spirituality that aligns with concerns about pollution, global warming, deforestation, extinction, and other environmental woes, Wicca seems a perfect fit.

> **"People are realizing that there is more to this life than the mechanized culture in which we live."**

Perhaps the most surprising ally of Wicca has been secularism. Some scholars, including Rodney Stark and William Bainbridge, have described Wicca's success as a backlash against the growing secularization of the West "by a headlong plunge back into magic."[5] They maintain that the advance of secularism, and its impulse to expunge religious expression from the public square, has created a spiritual vacuum. Amid this dry secularity, Wicca offers an enticing alternative—a realm teeming with spells and spirits. Catherine Sanders agrees. She doesn't see people's attraction to Wicca merely as "a sign that people are interested in stranger and more bizarre things these days." Rather, she writes, "people are realizing that there is more to this life than the mechanized culture in which we live, and they want answers to quench the thirst in their souls."[6]

## MEET MORNINGHAWK

Ultimately, it is possible to know all about Wicca and the trends behind its incredible growth but still fail to understand how it attracts young people raised in the church. Now that we've seen Wicca from ten thousand feet, let's zoom in for a closer look.

Meet Morninghawk Apollo, a young husband and father who left the Christian faith of his youth to become a Wiccan. Of course Morninghawk Apollo is not his real name. In a common Wiccan practice, he renamed himself—a name he says was given to him in a dream by his spirit guide.

Morninghawk has a boyish face, and two long braided ponytails that hang well past his shoulders. His soft voice and measured words give him the air of an armchair psychiatrist. The demeanor no doubt serves him well in his role as a Wiccan priest who gives lessons on the craft for seekers and prison inmates. He and his young family live in southern California, and love engaging in Wiccan rituals together in public parks. When concerned park rangers approach, Morninghawk calms their fears with his kindness and transparency, breaking from circle formation to patiently explain the meaning of the candles, incense, and daggers used in their rituals.

Seeing Morninghawk clad in his Wiccan garb, it's difficult to imagine his rather ordinary Lutheran upbringing in Minnesota. Morninghawk describes his parents as "Christmas Christians," the kind of folks who attended church only once or twice a year. Morninghawk, however, was more involved. He was confirmed and became involved in the church's youth group. He still gushes about his youth pastor. "He was a big influence on me. He was the kind of guy you could talk to about anything."

An interest in theology led Morninghawk to read books by the radical liberal Episcopal bishop John Shelby Spong, whom he describes as "a huge influence." In college he became interested in studying the Bible, but not for devotional reasons, like the other Christians on campus. He was more interested in comparative religion and studying the Bible from "an academic perspective." Morninghawk's study eventually led him away from the faith altogether. For a time he was even agnostic. But the spiritual void was still there. When he walked into a bookstore one day and picked up a book on the history of Wicca, something clicked. "I had to buy it," he recalls. "Once I had it, I felt an urge to read it."

Soon he was seeking out other Wiccans to learn more about his newfound passion. Today he believes that picking up his first book on Wicca was no mistake. He was guided to that bookstore. But guided by whom?

"I didn't know," Morninghawk says. "I had to ask. That's when I met my spirit guide." Now Morninghawk communes with a number of spirit guides regularly through meditation.

And what came of his agnostic skepticism?

Morninghawk embraced the supernatural after a momentous encounter with a Wiccan priest. "In my particular tradition, we have a practice that is similar to possession, where a god or goddess can enter a person's body and he or she can speak as an oracle," Morninghawk explained. "I know that some people can con you, by sizing you up and telling you things about your life," he said. "But this was different. When one of the gods was speaking through the priest, he told me specific things about my early childhood, about events that happened, things I've never told anyone about." Morninghawk was sold. "Even if the priest was really good at reading people, he wouldn't have been able to do that!"

Morninghawk discusses his rejection of Christianity with surprising candor. "Ultimately why I left is that Yahweh, the Christian God, demands that you submit to His will. In Wiccan faith, it's just the other way around. Your will is paramount. We believe in gods and serve gods, but the deities we choose to serve are based on our will."

He is equable when discussing Christianity. "I see the Christian God as just one of many gods. I see Jesus as very wise, a very old soul. He's lived many lifetimes. I put Him on the same level as Muhammad and the Dalai Lama." Morninghawk also concedes, "I haven't been treated too badly by Christians."

However, he acknowledges that his calm attitude toward Christian faith is the exception in Wiccan circles. "I see a lot of people running from Christianity, a lot of anger and hate toward Christians" he says.

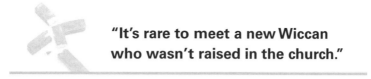

### "It's rare to meet a new Wiccan who wasn't raised in the church."

He also reports that Wicca is having tremendous success with younger people from Christian backgrounds. "The new ones are in their teens or twenties. Almost all of them were raised Christian. In fact, it's rare to meet a new Wiccan who wasn't raised in the church."

I have to admit that Morninghawk's story left me shaken.

Grappling with the phenomenon of deconversion is difficult enough; encountering people who leave for Wicca, a religion that I regard as dangerous and even demonic, is downright troubling. Yet I believe it's essential we listen to such stories. We need to understand new religions like Wicca, and why so many raised in the church are embracing its beliefs and practices.

## BRAVE NEO-PAGAN WORLD

Wicca's success has not been confined to secret covens. Witch-craft has penetrated the wider culture. Just think of the deluge of TV shows such as *Bewitched* and *Charmed*, movies like *The Craft* and *Practical Magic*, and even the wildly popular *Harry Potter* books. A trip to my local Wal-Mart was telling. Out of the 104 books on the bestseller rack, 39 had pagan themes, with titles that included *The Sorceress* and *Witch and Wizard*. The ubiquity of witchcraft in entertainment testifies to the fact that paganism has successfully made the journey from scary subculture to main-stream cool.

But while Wicca has a powerful appeal with members of the younger generation, most will never invoke the Wiccan goddess or participate in pagan rituals. But that doesn't mean they won't be affected by neo-paganism. There is a popular current of neo-pagan thought that is not explicitly tied to any religion but that is never-theless leading many away from the Christian faith of their youth. It venerates the earth as spiritual mother, lowers humans to the level of animals, and denies the reality of a holy, transcendent God.

I attended college in Portland, Oregon, a city notorious for its celebration of earth-based spirituality. For every Jesus fish you see on a car bumper in Portland, you're likely to spot several that read "Born Again Pagan," "Dirt Worshiper" or "Blessed Be," the standard Wiccan blessing. Though I was an English major, my interest in environmental issues led me to take classes such as Global Ecology and Ecocriticism. But I was in for a surprise. I had signed up for more than an education about the wonders of nature. At times it felt more like Paganism 101.

It started with the language we were encouraged to use. In one class, the word "animals" was considered taboo. Instead we were instructed to refer to our four-legged friends as either "earth others" or as "more-than-human," which was our professor's moniker of choice. The course's central text was *The Spell of the Sensuous* by David Abram, an ecological writer whose beautiful prose gushes with praise for Balinese and Nepalese shamans and their animistic beliefs. Abram argues that our estrangement from nature came through the Judeo-Christian focus on the written word. "Only as the written text began to speak would the voices of the forest, and of the river, begin to fade," writes Abram.

Other attacks on Christian faith were even more overt. The first chapter of Genesis, I learned, was a dangerous script. God's command to Adam to "take dominion over the earth" provided the western world with the justification it needed to destroy the environment. I was perplexed by such a reading of the Bible's first book. I was raised to cherish and protect creation precisely because it was God's creation. Apparently I had it all backward. Humans were not the apex of God's creation. They were on par with animals, or even beneath them, since we had done so much to destroy our terrestrial brothers. The Bible's teaching that we are ontologically superior to animals and that God is above and outside the material world was deemed unacceptable. True spirituality, it was implied, reveres the earth, and eschews our cherished theories of transcendence.

My wife, who attended the same college, took a class on the subject of faith. Instead of studying the great religious traditions of the world, students were shown films such as *What the Bleep*

*Do We Know?* a "docudrama" that claims water has conscious-
ness, that "we are all gods in the making," and that a theistic understanding of God is "ugly, superstitious, backwater." The popular
documentary was directed and funded by students of guru J. Z.
Knight, a woman who claims to channel a 35,000-year-old deity.
They also watched a documentary about culturally insensitive
missionaries, prompting one student to comment afterward, "My
family always gave money to the missionaries that came to our
church. Now I feel really bad. We just didn't know."

It's important to note that in these classes, Christian faith was
not attacked for its supernatural claims. It wasn't skeptical atheists leading the charge. Rather, Christianity as being critiqued
from essentially a neo-pagan perspective. It was derided because
it was not earth-centered, it taught that humanity was the crown
of creation, and it revealed a God both immanent and transcendent. It's also crucial to note that this kind of thinking is not confined to liberal arts colleges in progressive cities like Portland. In
the five years since I graduated from college, I've encountered
these ideas repeatedly, in multiple cities, and almost always among
members of the younger generation.

# II- Engaging Neo-Pagans

As you can probably already tell, my college wasn't exactly a friendly place for Christians. The school paper rarely addressed religious topics, so I remember being surprised to pick up an edition one day and see Michelangelo's "The Creation of Adam" frame from the Sistine Chapel splashed across the lead page. I had seen the sprawling, cosmic depiction so many times that initially I failed to notice that the newspaper had altered the picture. While God's majestic form was the same, with one arm extending through the heavens down to His creation, Adam had been significantly changed. Instead of holding his hand out tenderly toward God, he was making a gesture at the Creator.

Though I found this distortion offensive, I had to admit that the parody did encapsulate the prevailing attitude on campus. Days earlier, sitting at a campus café, I'd overheard a lively conversation at the table next to me. Two professors were discussing a variety of topics, when one statement caught my attention. "I hate Christianity," one of them said, turning suddenly pensive and looking out the window. "I really hate it." I stared into my coffee cup, awaiting his reasoning, but none was given. The other professor simply nodded his agreement and the conversation moved on.

**What gave me pause was the white-hot anger that often smoldered just behind their words.**

I was stunned by this hostility, and at times, immobilized. When Christianity came under fire in my classes I tried to speak up, but too often I was silent. The arguments being leveled against the faith weren't difficult to counter. Typically they were laughable, making me wonder whether the detractors had even read the Bible or any church history. I almost felt sorry for the sophomore girl I interrupted to inform that the earliest Christians did not—as she so ardently claimed—participate in the Crusades. It was not the arguments I heard that stalled me. Rather, what gave me pause was the white-hot anger that often smoldered just behind their words. It wasn't the substance of their arguments; it was their temperature. Passion is intimidating, and sometimes I just didn't feel up to the fight.

I think the same dynamic is present when it comes to speaking to many leavers about God. Most have harsh words for the very beliefs that you cherish. It's uncomfortable to hear, and it's difficult to confront. Add to this the fact that many of us just aren't built for conflict. Our voices shake. Our hands tremble. Blood rushes to our faces, and our eyes fill with tears involuntarily.

## LISTEN AND UNDERSTAND

When it comes to talking with neo-pagans, the problem only amplifies. Judging from my experience, neo-pagan leavers have *the strongest emotional reaction* to Christian faith. They're not the most apt to argue—modernist leavers take that prize—but once they open up to you, be ready for a river of molten rage. The first step is simply bracing for this charged emotion. But you can weather the vitriol and engage them in meaningful conversations about God.

Why do Wiccans have such negative feelings toward Christianity? The reason is no mystery: we have repeatedly twisted and misrepresented their beliefs. We've called them Satan-worshipers, accused them of sacrificing animals (a practice that would directly contradict their worship of nature), and even spread rumors that they ritualistically murder babies. Understandably, they become angry when they encounter these kinds of wild misperceptions.

The first step in defusing these negative feelings is to demonstrate a familiarity with their basic beliefs. They will find this refreshing and be more open to listen to what you have to say later. Ask them questions about what attracted them to Wicca in the first place. Not only will you discover more about their beliefs; you will likely hear some of the specific problems they have with Christianity as well.

## CARE FOR CREATION

The biblical narrative opens in a paradisiacal garden and ends with the stunning image of the heavenly Eden, a city with trees, precious stones, and a river "as clear as crystal." Given the prominence of nature in the Bible, and God's clear command to steward the earth, it's something of a scandal that Christians are seen as being anti-environment. Of course there's a reason we've been slow to jump on the environmental bandwagon. As I discovered in my college ecology classes, many environmentalists mingle their activism with neo-pagan beliefs. And we Christians rightly refuse to do the same. We don't extol the earth as a sentient being (think Gaia) or worship it as our spiritual mother, so our knee-jerk reaction is to reject the causes championed by those who do. Unfortunately, in our age of wanton environmental degradation, creation care is vitally important, and completely consistent with Christian principles. It's also essential to our witness, especially to neo-pagans.

Neo-pagans sense something sacred in nature, and they are not mistaken. The Bible describes creation as a reflection of the Creator.

> For ever since the world was created, people have seen the earth and sky. Through everything God made, they can clearly see his invisible qualities—his eternal power and divine nature. So they have no excuse for not knowing God. (Romans 1:20)

When a Wiccan ventures into a mossy forest at twilight seeking a divine encounter, she won't be disappointed, because, as the poet Gerard Manley Hopkins wrote, "The world is charged with the grandeur of God." She senses something real. Her mistake is not that she goes too far; it's that she doesn't go far enough. She stops short and bows before what she encounters, rather than directing her worship to the true source of nature's awe-inspiring power, God.

But neo-pagans will reject any spirituality that fails to account for the sacredness they've encountered in creation. Respect their experience by expressing and demonstrating care for the environment. Reaching neo-pagans begins with showing an appreciation for nature and a desire to protect it, all while directing them to the God of whom nature is a grand reflection.

## HONOR EVE

There's a clever Wiccan bumper sticker and T-shirt that simply reads, "Eve was framed!" This humorous slogan reveals a serious beef many neo-pagans have with the Christian faith. In *Wicca's Charm*, Sanders reports that many of the Wiccan women she interviewed left Christianity because they felt undervalued in the church. "Their gifts had been confined to teaching Sunday school and making coffee," Sanders writes. Such women found themselves drawn to neo-pagan religions that promised to honor their presence and utilize their gifts. While Sanders concludes that Wicca ultimately offers women a false dignity, she wonders how much better the church has done. "Do women need to go outside the church to find a religion, such as neo-paganism, that celebrates their womanhood?" she asks.

The gender issue looms large for neo-pagan leavers, whether they're women or men. It will surface quickly in any conversation you have with them about your faith. They commonly report growing up in "Christian" environments where women were treated as second class-citizens, or even outright abused. When they talk to you, they'll be listening carefully to see if you're different. How do you speak about women and their role in religion? Are you dismissive of the issue? Do you acknowledge the historical injustices done to women, even those perpetrated in the name of God? If such questions aren't acknowledged and addressed, they will continue to believe that Christians are not serious about honoring women.

In your conversations with neo-pagan leavers, highlight women in ministry. Speak enthusiastically about the programs and activities at your church that are geared specifically toward fostering spiritual growth in the lives of women. And, of course, point to the compelling example of Jesus, who always related to women in a way that was gentle, yet never demeaning. After spending a year interacting with neo-pagans, Sanders recalls, "No one had a bad word to say about Him (Jesus) during my research. Ever. Talking about Jesus is always a great conversation starter with neo-Pagans."

## SHARE SPIRITUAL EXPERIENCES

A week after my neighbor Lisa announced her plans to attend a Wiccan maypole dance, my wife had an idea. "Let's invite Lisa to our small group meeting!" she said. The group was meeting in our apartment that week, so Lisa could just walk over from next door. Usually our meetings involved a time of sharing and a short Bible study, but we were planning something different for that Wednesday: a prayer meeting.

"I don't know," I told my wife. "Maybe it would be better to have her come on a different night." I wasn't sure that listening to a dozen people pray would be the best way to introduce her to our group. The prayer would be spirited and intense. I was worried that she might feel intimidated or turned off in the midst of such an overt and intimate spiritual activity.

Despite my reservations we invited Lisa and she agreed to come. On Wednesday night we crowded into our small apartment living room. The members of the group introduced themselves to Lisa and made her feel welcome. When it came time to share requests, Lisa offered several. Afterward, I noticed that her eyes were red. "It was so meaningful to have someone pray for me," she said. She wasn't scared off by prayer. Far from it. Watching Christians passionately petitioning God was exactly what she needed to see. Shortly after that night, Lisa showed up at our door. Her grandfather had passed away suddenly, and she asked us to pray over her. That night of prayer had made an impact, and opened the door for other conversations about God.

**Neo-Pagans do not worship the devil, but their forays into the spiritual realm are hardly innocuous.**

Those who leave the faith for neo-pagan religions often regard Christian spirituality as a dry and dusty affair. Too often the Christianity they've known was really dead religion, devoid of the power of God's Spirit. It's up to you to dispel that perception. So don't be shy about talking about your spiritual experiences with neo-pagans. And don't make the same mistake that I did, assuming that they'll be turned off by expressions of overt Christian spirituality. They are usually the kind of people who prize experience over theory, and who embrace spiritual truth with their hearts before they'll accept it with their minds. Only when they witness believers in dynamic and authentic worship of God will they begin to wonder whether Christians have the right answers. My grand-father always says that spiritual truth is learned through atmosphere. This is definitely true for neo-pagans. If they can sense the presence of God in your midst, they just may begin their journey back to the fold.

## PRAY!

Neo-pagans do not worship the devil, but their forays into the spiritual realm are hardly innocuous. I believe that many, like Morninghawk, invoke powers they cannot understand or control. Satan is real, and he uses neo-paganism to hold people in bondage and keep them from relationships with the one true God. Any attempt to reach these leavers must take account of this spiritual reality.

Realize that the battle is spiritual at its core. Spend time in the presence of God before speaking to neo-pagans. Ask God to bind spiritual powers that may be preventing His prodigal children from returning home. Ultimately, they won't come back to God because of your words or actions; God must move in their hearts. Only the Father of lights can dispel darkness. Once He does, the best we can hope to do is gently lead them home.

# Profile of a NEO-PAGAN

Lucy is twenty-three, and lives with her boyfriend, Jack. They own a California king snake named Big Boy, a Chilean rose-haired tarantula named Crimson, and a Red-footed tortoise named Fred. Oh, and a pit bull named Apollo. She has twenty-six piercings and twelve tattoos, including one of a giant koi fish that covers half her left arm.

By looking at her, you probably wouldn't guess that Lucy grew up in a Christian family, but she did. At church she enjoyed the singing—and that was about it.

"I didn't really understand any of it," she recalls. "I felt like church was useless."

When she turned to her parents for answers, they didn't seem interested in providing them.

"They wouldn't tell me why we were going to this place every Sunday. I think it's ridiculous to make children do something that you can't explain."

Lucy's older sister, however, was eager to share her growing interest in Wicca. She handed Lucy a copy of *Teen Witch*, by Silver Ravenwolf, a Wiccan classic.

Lucy was hooked. "I loved how natural Wicca was. Even at twelve years old I could understand the concepts. The idea of equality also really appealed to me. As I read more about Wicca, I knew I didn't want to be a Christian anymore."

Today Lucy describes herself as a "solitary witch."

"I may not cast spells, but I love the natural aspects of Wicca. I don't need a building to practice my faith. I can do Wicca anywhere."

The topic of church is still a sore spot, she says. "I still think church is useless. Some churches even require patrons to give a percentage of their paychecks just to keep the building nice. What a ridiculous concept! I'd never pay money to practice my faith. Never."

In Lucy's eyes, the Bible doesn't fare much better than church. When asked her opinion of Jesus, she responds, "I honestly don't have an opinion of Jesus. I don't trust the Bible. It isn't exactly the best vessel for truth. I cannot believe in something that has been rewritten many times over the years to better suit Christians."

Lucy sees an agenda behind this alleged rewriting.

"They spent a lot of time rewriting the Bible so they could make people hate witches," she says. "They say that Wiccans believe in the devil. But Christianity created the devil, so how can witches worship it? It's like a form of racism."

Lucy's advice for Christians is equally outspoken. "Stop being such hypocrites! Stop being so quick to condemn everything," she says. "You say you're all about forgiveness and getting along. But when something is new and different you're the first ones screaming about how evil it is. Everyone is entitled to their opinions. Everyone. Not just you."

# Section 5

## Rebels

# 12- Party Time

Next to Billy Graham, Luis Palau is likely the most prominent evangelist on the planet. Over his fifty-eight-year career, the Argentinean-born evangelist has preached in seventy-two countries, ministered to one billion people, and registered more than one million decisions to accept Jesus Christ. He's authored nearly fifty books, and his radio broadcasts, in both English and Spanish, are heard on over 2,600 radio stations all over the world. In recent years Palau has also become an unlikely catalyst for social change in Portland, Oregon, where he lives. He's partnered with the city's openly gay mayor to mobilize the local church to help feed the homeless.

With those kinds of Christian credentials, you might assume that Palau's children would be zealous Christians—and you'd be right. Indeed, today three of Palau's sons serve alongside their father in ministry. But things weren't always that way. Palau's son, Andrew, spent years away from God before returning at the age of twenty-seven. His famous evangelist father found himself in the same painful place of so many other Christian parents: wondering if his prodigal would ever return.

How could someone raised by Luis Palau wander from the faith? Did Andrew have an intellectual crisis? Did he suffer a traumatic event? Was he lured away by another religion?

None of the above.

According to him, the reason for his prodigal phase wasn't all that complicated. "I just really loved to party!" Andrew says. "People say, 'I know why you rebelled. Your father was probably shoving his religion down your throat.'"

Andrew chuckles at such conclusions. "Hey, I wish I could say I had an excuse like that, but that just wasn't the case."

In fact, Andrew has fond memories of growing up in the home of an evangelist. "My parents loved us. Like anyone, they weren't perfect, but they practiced what they preached. They were dedicated to their ministry, but they made us the priority."

And, of course, Andrew was exposed to the gospel early on. "I knew the truth," he says. "I wasn't shaking my fist at God. I was just following the path of least resistance."

Andrew confesses embarrassment over such overtly hedonistic motives. "The reasons that some other people leave are a lot more credible," he says. "I'm ashamed to say that I just wanted to do my own thing. I wanted to smoke dope with my buddies and chase women. I was driven by self-gratification."

It wasn't always easy being a black sheep in a prominent evangelical family. Though Andrew tried to escape notice, his parents and Christian friends sought him out to talk about the state of his spiritual life.

"I wouldn't lie and say everything was cool, but I would try to avoid the conflict and get out of the situation as quickly as possible," Andrew remembers. "I'd try to convince the person they'd made enough of a difference to leave me alone. I just weaseled my way out of those kinds of conversations."

Fittingly, it was at an evangelistic rally in Jamaica (which he attended at his father's request) that Andrew surrendered to God. "I had a moment of radical transformation, a 180-degree turnaround," he says.

Today Andrew is becoming a successful evangelist in his own right, and he still looks back with awe at his unlikely journey.

"When you're away from God you think, *It's too late for me. I will lose all my friends. I won't have any fun.*" Andrew laughs again. "It's amazing the lies you believe."

## MORAL COMPROMISE REVISITED

In chapter 1, we considered a common assumption: that young people leave the faith because they are unwilling to adhere to Christian morality. I wrote that this assumption is sometimes wrong, and that moral compromise doesn't always tell the whole story. As we've examined the diverse stories of real-world leavers, I hope you can see why I came to that conclusion.

**Why suffer under strict ethical standards when the warm waters of moral laxity beckon?**

Yet my caveat should not overshadow the fact that moral compromise often does play a role. Sometimes it's a central role. For leavers like Andrew, it serves as the primary reason for their departure. Andrew didn't have doubts about the faith. For him, the bottom line was autonomy. "I loved the sin that I was engaged in," he told me. "I'd built my foundation for life on it, and it was hard to turn away."

Many are in the same boat. They simply find Christianity too demanding. Why suffer under strict ethical standards when the warm waters of moral laxity beckon? For thousands of young people, the answer is a no-brainer.

Moral compromise also affects the kinds of leavers we've already discussed. For a young person dealing with doubts or hurt by Christians, the lure of sinful activities makes alternatives to Christian faith look all the more appealing. In these cases, moral rebellion becomes a powerful secondary reason for leaving the faith.

## MY BROTHER'S STORY

Three years ago, I received a frantic late-night phone call from my mom. Between sobs, she informed me that my brother Dave was in trouble. He was being held hostage by gang members.

"They're holding a gun to his head!" my mom cried.

My mind spun with confusion as I tried to make sense of her words. I knew my brother had been having trouble, but not *this* kind of trouble.

Only a couple years earlier, Dave had been a paragon of success. He was married with two children, earned a multiple six-figure income, and lived in a large house in an upscale neighborhood—all before reaching thirty years old. But private sins were peeling back the façade. A gambling addiction destroyed his finances. A porn problem led to infidelity and cost him his marriage. He lost his house and his business too. "Sin will take you further than you want to go," goes a popular saying. "It will keep you longer than you want to stay, and it will cost you more than you want to pay." Dave's life became a tragic fulfillment of that maxim.

I was saddened by these developments yet hoped Dave's devastating reversal of fortunes would serve a purpose—to bring him back to God. Not that he'd ever explicitly left. He hadn't disavowed his faith or anything like that. If you had cornered Dave and asked him to affirm the doctrines of the Christian faith, he would have gladly obliged. But his life told a different story. Gone was the ardent faith he'd possessed as a teenager who went on mission trips and led Bible studies for our youth group. Now when God was mentioned, he seemed to shut down. But he grew animated when he talked about driving a Ferrari, wearing Armani suits, or his plans to become a billionaire.

**When God was mentioned, he seemed to shut down.**

When Dave's life unraveled, we prayed for a silver lining. Surely the loss of his family and career would be the wakeup call that he needed.

We were wrong. Instead Dave only plunged deeper into the sins that had messed up his life in the first place. The club crowd became his new social circle. He emailed me pictures of himself surrounded by tattooed bodybuilders and scantily clad women. I barely recognized my brother in the photos. His skin was tanned and his hair was bleached blond. He'd traded his business attire for skinny jeans, and an open shirt that revealed a gaudy chain dangling around his neck.

I had no problem with his new look, but the life that accompanied it was anything but innocent. He started doing hard drugs, and making friends with drug dealers. Within months he'd talked himself into the inner circle of a multimillion-dollar drug cartel. Since Dave had no criminal history, the gang used him to pick up drugs and transport suitcases of cash. Dave was participating in highly illegal activities, but his ultimate confrontation would not be with the law. It turned out that his new "friends" weren't that friendly when he borrowed $14,000 and failed to repay them.

That's when we got the call from Dave as he was held at gunpoint. After an agonizing two days, which included repeated threats to Dave and our family, he was released. He had twenty-four hours to get the money, he was told, or he would be killed. But Dave feared he'd be killed even if he did pay up, so we put him on a plane and got him out of the country. He didn't come back for a year.

The whole episode left my family badly shaken, not only by Dave's near-death experience, but by his sudden moral descent. It was hard to believe that a lust problem and a penchant for material possessions could lead him down such a dangerous path. As I witnessed Dave's life become a waking nightmare, I couldn't help thinking of James's haunting words, penned nearly two thousand years ago: "Then when lust has conceived, it gives birth to sin; and when sin is accomplished, it brings forth death."

When Dave returned, he agreed to a yearlong Christian rehabilitation program to deal with his destructive addictions. Though I feel Dave truly renewed his faith in Christ and addressed his vices, he still struggles. Since completing the program he has fallen back into his old habits more than once. We continue to pray for him. To this day, his battle continues.

## FALLOUT

Dave's painful journey taught me at least two crucial lessons. First, that falling away from God does not require denying Him with your words. Like many leavers, my brother never bothered to verbally renounce his faith. Yet his actions showed an unmistakable departure from the faith. Second, it showed me that such stories do not play out in a vacuum. Dave's actions hurt every person who loved him.

As I prepared to write this book, I read up on the literature on "deconversion." I learned a lot about the many factors that contribute to the phenomenon of leaving the faith. Yet at the same time, reading these studies felt somewhat surreal. The detached, academic tone of the material seemed incongruous when applied to the intimate issue of personal faith. Social scientists write about people walking away from God as if observing caribou migrate across the Alaskan tundra.

> **We feel perplexed by the choices of our loved ones and powerless to turn them around.**

For most of us, the issue is very different. We have witnessed a family member or friend walk away from God. It's not something we observe dispassionately from a safe distance. Our interest isn't academic. It impacts us personally. It's devastating. We feel perplexed by the choices of our loved ones and powerless to turn them around. When they leave for moral reasons, it can be even more difficult to talk to them. If their objections were intellectual, we could reason with them. But what happens when the cause of their departure is simply an assertion of will? How do you rescue someone borne away on the tide of their own desires? How do you argue with the heart?

# 13- Rebels

So far we've discussed four kinds of leavers: postmodernists, recoilers, modernists, and neo-pagans. These categories emerged as I interacted with leavers and attempted to identify, in broad terms, the essential reasons that they left the faith. These groupings are not meant to be scientifically precise; their value is diagnostic and utilitarian. In other words, they should help you to determine why people abandon the faith, and then sharpen your efforts to reach them. Armed with an understanding of why they left, you'll be better equipped to address their specific concerns and lead them back.

## MORAL REBELS

Next, we look at a new category: "Rebels." Unlike the other categories, "Rebels" includes two kinds of leavers. The first I call "moral rebels." Like the leavers we encountered in the last chapter, moral rebels forsake the faith to indulge in sinful behaviors. The fact that this often happens in early adulthood shouldn't surprise us. As young adults wrestle free of their parents' authority, they find a host of new freedoms and corresponding temptations. Curfews disappear. Rules evaporate. Sexual temptations abound. For those without a strong grounding in the faith, resisting the onslaught can feel futile. It's no coincidence that more people abandon Christianity between the ages of eighteen and twenty-two than during any other four years of life.[1]

The moral rebel makes repeated appearances in Scripture, most famously in what's commonly called "the parable of the prodigal son." In Jesus' story, the younger of the two sons demands his inheritance early from their father.

Why such a rash decision? Presumably, for no other reason than to fund his party lifestyle: "The younger son got together all he had, set off for a distant country and there squandered his wealth in wild living" (Luke 15:13). After the younger son "comes to his senses" and returns home to a forgiving father, the clean-living older son is incensed. He rails against the father's generosity, and brings details of his brother's "wild living" to light. "But when this son of yours who has squandered your property *with prostitutes* comes home, you kill the fattened calf for him!" (Luke 15:30, emphasis mine.)

Of course, this story isn't about an earthly father; it's about a heavenly One. And though the pithy parable is loaded with lessons, one takeaway is almost jarringly simple: sometimes people leave God merely to fulfill sinful desires.

A coworker of mine recently expressed concern about her own prodigal son. "He came right out and told me that he believes in God," she said. "He even says that he feels God calling him. But he's unwilling to live the Christian life right now."

Andrew Palau believes that a lot of young ex-Christians are in the same boat. "I think the vast majority are like I was," he says.

"You know, just punk kids who are self-motivated."

Andrew's right. I remember one friend of mine who was blatant about his hedonistic motivations for ditching his faith. Though he held Christian beliefs, he wasn't willing to give up his serial promiscuity or illegal activities. And he wasn't worried about spiritual repercussions. He had a plan. "I'll clean up my act if I see the end times coming," he told me, without a trace of irony. "That way I can have my fun and then repent just before Jesus comes back."

## SPIRITUAL REBELS

The second category of rebels I've termed "spiritual rebels." These people rebel, not against the Christian lifestyle, but against the very authority of God. Submitting to an all-powerful deity is an idea they find intolerable.

> **"If there's a God, that means He's over me and I can't handle that."**

I will never forget my tenth-grade English teacher. He was notoriously anti-Christian, and used his lectern as a bully pulpit to instill atheistic beliefs. One day after another screed against Christianity, he shared his "ultimate reason" for rejecting the faith. Through gritted teeth he told the class, "If there's a God, that means He's over me and I can't handle that."

Even to my fifteen-year-old mind, his warped logic was apparent. Just because you don't like the idea of a God, doesn't mean He doesn't exist. Yet amazingly, in recent years, this kind of naked defiance has passed for a valid argument against God's existence.

In a 2008 debate on the issue of God's existence, popular atheist Christopher Hitchens railed against the idea of a superintend-
ing deity. "It's a horrible idea that there's someone who made us,
who owns us," Hitchens said. "To accept God is to live as abject
slaves." For Hitchens and his many disciples, there's only one
appropriate response to such a ruling power. "This belief in a
Supreme Being is the oldest enemy of our species," he said. "It
must be met and must be challenged and must be overthrown."

To start the debate, Hitchens's Christian counterpart presented
seven detailed arguments for God's existence. But when Hitchens
stood to speak he seemed uninterested in refuting these arguments or providing any of his own. Instead, turning to the audience
he said, "I don't think there's *any* form of persuasion that should
convince you to be spoken to as if you were serfs or slaves." In
other words, it didn't matter how compelling the arguments for
God's existence were. They must be rejected out of hand because
the idea of God's authority was simply too dreadful to accept.

I spoke with a young woman who had lost her faith while
attending a prominent Christian college. While her classmates
deepened their walks with God, doubts were multiplying like
weeds in her mind, choking her faith. She had reservations about
the doctrine of the Trinity. She objected to the apostle Paul's teachings. The presence of multiple Christian denominations was also
a stumbling block. "There are so many different churches. How can
you tell who is right?" she asked.

Toward the end of our conversation she offered a critique
that piqued my curiosity. She found the story of Lazarus' resurrection particularly troublesome. I thought that was an odd story
to find offensive. After all, it's a story that showcases Jesus' power
and sympathy. Even most skeptics can't help feeling drawn by the
Servant Messiah who stopped to weep with the mourners outside
Lazarus' tomb. Not her. She found the story repulsive. "Why did

He let Lazarus die?" she asked. "Jesus knew he was sick. Jesus had already demonstrated that He could heal from a distance."

"So it's Jesus' perceived lack of compassion that bothers you?" I asked.

"No," she said. "I think Jesus was trying to show off. He wouldn't heal Lazarus from a distance because He wanted to do perform a more miraculous feat by raising him from the dead."

I was confused. Moments ago she had called herself an atheist. Now she was angry about how Jesus used His supernatural powers?

"Well," I said. "You don't actually believe that Jesus raised Lazarus anyway, right?"

"Even if I did, I wouldn't follow Him," she replied.

Her statement took me aback. "Let me get this straight," I said. "If you had irrefutable proof of Jesus' miracles, and that God existed, you still wouldn't be a Christian?"

Her response was chilling.

"I'd rather burn in hell," she said, laughing. "I'd *gladly* burn in hell."

Suddenly I saw her deconversion in a whole new light. Her denial of God had little to do with intellectual doubts. After all, she admitted that not even undeniable evidence could persuade her to return. Her true obstacle was sheer spiritual rebellion. She would rather burn in hell than bend her knee.

As she spoke, I couldn't help hear the echo from Luke 19:14: "We will not have this man to reign over us." That was the cry of the unfaithful servants in the parable Jesus aimed at the Pharisees, a group of religious leaders, who had witnessed His miraculous power and yet denied His lordship. Today the same cry rings out from many exiting the faith. Deep down they may believe, but they're too proud to bow. Where God extends a loving hand, they raise defiant fists.

# 14- Rebels Needing a Cause

My childhood church had a beautiful custom. Each time a person accepted Jesus, we would lay a solitary red rose on the sanctuary altar. The symbolism was simple yet elegant. What better than a rose to represent the beauty and freshness of a new life in Christ?

My dad was the pastor. When a rose was laid on the altar, he would explain the meaning of our little practice.

"The joy we are experiencing here is just a small taste of the celebration that's happening in heaven," he would say. Then he would read Luke 15:7: "I tell you that in the same way there will be more rejoicing in heaven over one sinner who repents than over ninety-nine righteous persons who do not need to repent."

When I heard that verse, my young mind strained to imagine what a heavenly celebration would be like. Would the angels dance? Could celestial singing be heard on the streets of gold? Did God Himself let loose a thunderous shout of joy?

I still get excited when I hear about someone coming

to faith in Christ. Unfortunately, these days, it seems like the reverse happens more, and I hear of yet another person who has walked away. I know I'm not alone. Millions of Christians grapple with the same reality. Instead of celebrating, too often we find ourselves confused and reeling with grief. Rather than rejoicing with the angels, we're engulfed by earthly sadness. What happened? And how should we respond?

## BEWARE FIRST IMPULSES

With moral rebels, controlling our initial impulses is crucial. They may not renounce their faith verbally, but as the saying goes, actions speak louder than words. And those actions get your attention. When my brother walked away, there was no ignoring it. When we see moral rebels engaging in sinful activities, our natural instinct is to intervene, and even command them to stop. Sometimes this is appropriate, especially when those around them are placed in immediate danger. But too often we jump into arguments homing in on their offending moral behaviors.

> **Moral rebels will tune you out, depriving you of future opportunities to speak into their lives.**

This is particularly tempting for parents of leavers. It's difficult to hold your tongue when you witness your son or daughter making destructive choices. However, decrying their sins is not only futile, it can actually be counterproductive. Moral rebels will tune you out, depriving you of future opportunities to speak into their lives. In a cruel twist of irony your natural desire to save them from poor choices can in fact push them further away. Instead, speak to them about the core issue: the state of their relationship with God. That's what underlies their sinful behavior. Unless there's a florescence in their spiritual life, any behavior changes you convince them to make will be minor and temporary anyway.

A second knee-jerk reaction is completely different, but just as harmful: not to respond at all. Some Christians comfort themselves with the false belief that the spiritual plight of moral rebels is not really so serious. When Andrew Palau was away from the faith, some well-meaning Christians tried to comfort his mother. "Oh, he's just a good all-American kid. He's sowing his wild oats. It's not a big deal," they said.

> ## "What in my son's life do you see that suggests he's a born-again Christian?"

Mrs. Palau's response was polite but direct. "I hate to be negative," she told them, "but I have to face the reality if I'm going to respond appropriately to it. What in my son's life do you see that suggests he's a born-again Christian?"

Her response to her friends may sound harsh, but Andrew believes it was her insistence on taking a clear-eyed view of his spiritual plight that enabled her to speak meaningfully into his life. "When young people rebel with their lifestyle, but don't come out and challenge Christian beliefs, it's easy to get stuck in denial that they ever really left," Andrew says. "My mom refused to say her son was fine. But that didn't make her respond negatively. In fact it caused her to be more proactive about reaching out to me." Andrew's father was similarly realistic. "God has no grandchildren, only children," Andrew recalls his father saying, emphasizing the need for each generation to discover God afresh.

## GIVE THEM A CAUSE!

So far we haven't talked much about the role that the church has played in the departure of young adults. Some have overstated the case against the church, pinning the full responsibility of the trend on Christian hypocrisy and flawed ministry approaches. While I'm wary of such categorical condemnations, this one contains at least a kernel of truth. And where we've been part of the problem, we must acknowledge our complicity.

In the 1980s business thinking took the church by storm, changing the way many congregations in North America did ministry. Perhaps nowhere was the impact felt more profoundly than in youth programs. Instead of placing the emphasis on discipleship, the focus shifted to attracting large numbers of kids and keeping them entertained. Not necessarily bad goals, but they've had some ugly unintended consequences. Today many youth ministries are practically devoid of any spiritual engagement. Some have been reduced to using violent video game parties to lure students through their church doors on Friday nights.[1] Church researcher Ed Stetzer describes most youth groups as "holding tanks with pizza." Recently I asked Josh Riebock, author of *mY Generation*, to solve a riddle for me: why are so many teenagers, who were active in youth group, leaving the faith after high school? His response was simple. "Let's face it," he said. "There are a lot more fun things to do at college than eat pizza."

As we fired up the fun in youth ministry, we watered down the gospel. Many have adopted that mentality, but it's only succeeded in making the gospel boring. I remember listening in horror as a speaker from a large youth ministry spoke to a room full of high school students. "Becoming a Christian isn't hard," he said. "You won't have to change stuff. You won't lose your friends. Your life will be the same, just better." Maybe his words would have slipped by me if they hadn't been such obvious reversals of Jesus' own warnings about the hardships of following Him. Fortunately the teenagers weren't even listening. Why should they? I wondered. Who cares about a gospel that involves no adventure, no sacrifice, and no risk? It was a message reinforced by the local Christian radio station which repeatedly promised "safe, easy listening with no offensive lyrics." Again I couldn't help notice the advertisement's stark contrast to Jesus' warning about the offensiveness of His message or the disciples' complaint, "This is a hard teaching. Who can follow it?"

> **They don't want pizza and video games. They want revolution and dynamism.**

This brings me to an important point about moral rebels. Underneath their propensity for rebellious behavior lies a deep thirst for adventure and purpose. Often they're the kind of people with an irrepressible desire to live life to the fullest, even if that means taking risks. Unfortunately, when we present them with an eviscerated gospel, unworthy of their devotion, they seek to fulfill their desires in other ways.

It's a tragic development. Jim Rayburn, the founder of Young Life, liked to say, "It's a sin to bore a kid with the gospel." That mentality has actually led to entertainment numbness and resulted in a boring gospel. Somehow we thought we could water down the message for young people and make it easier for them to swallow, but it turns out that they're choking on our concoction. They don't want cute slogans and serenity. They don't want pizza and video games. They want revolution and dynamism. They want unvarnished truth. They want a cause to live and die for. In other words, they want the true gospel. When we present that gospel, with all its hard demands and radical implications, we'll finally be speaking the language moral rebels long to hear.

## LOOK FOR "MOMENTS OF HEIGHTENED RECEPTIVITY"

When I asked Andrew Palau how his parents broke through to him, he had difficulty narrowing it down. "Well, they did things nonstop," he said. They timed their vacations to match his so they could come and visit. "That made a big impact on me, because I knew they'd gone out of their way to see me," he said. And when they came to visit, they didn't preach at him. "They really focused on the relationship side of things. We just had a lot of fun when they came."

That doesn't mean they stayed silent on spiritual matters. "They never stopped sharing the good news with me. They brought it up in a hundred different ways. They gave me books, they asked people to talk to me. They brought me out to places where I'd be exposed to the gospel message." And there was something else. "They also looked for moments of heightened receptivity," Andrew recalls. "They knew that to recognize those moments, they had to be in prayer and sensitive to the Holy Spirit."

"Moments of heightened receptivity," Andrew explained, are those times when the circumstances in a person's life increase their spiritual openness. These are usually periods of turmoil and crisis. Often people reach out to God only when they hit rock bottom—a regrettable, but undeniable, tendency of human nature. The destructive lifestyles of moral rebels usually result in many times of turmoil and crisis. If we watch for these moments of heightened receptivity, and stay tuned to the Spirit's leading, we'll find numerous opportunities to engage moral rebels in meaningful conversations about God.

## SPIRITUAL REBELS

When I began researching ways to reach spiritual rebels— those leavers who simply defy God's authority—the results were disheartening. I don't have friends who fall into this category, and the ones I interviewed seemed cold, resolute, and generally unreachable. When I described this type of leaver to a thoughtful pastor, his initial response was dismal: "I don't think you can do anything," he told me.

The difficulty of reaching spiritual rebels underscores the importance of prayer. Prayer is paramount when it comes to reaching anyone who has left the faith, but when it comes to breaking through to those who shake their fists at God, it's especially important. Ultimately only God can soften their hearts and lead them back to Him. However, I do believe there are ways to clear the path for their return.

## EVERYONE SERVES SOMETHING

My wife recently attended a dinner party where a friend announced that religion was for "weak-minded people." The woman had seen a story on TV about people who were losing their homes in the foreclosure crisis and was cynical about what she saw as their naïve trust in God. "'Oh, I'll just trust God to save my house,'" she said. "'Everything will be fine.'"

My wife was rattled by the outburst. It seemed arbitrary and a little mean-spirited. Not only that, but this friend was well aware of our Christian faith. Did she mean to say that we too are weak-minded? As we reflected on her comments, we wondered what, if any, message she was trying to communicate. We also observed how her response was slightly ironic. Though she was repulsed by submission to God, she was busily serving her own master. It wasn't a divine master, but her devotion was every bit as intense. She was slavishly working to achieve the American dream. Perhaps her dedication to that goal explained her irritation with those who had failed to attain it.

We Christians are all too aware of this inescapable reality: everybody serves someone—or something. When we displace God, other masters arise to command our allegiance. As John Calvin said, "The human heart is an idol factory."

> **Spiritual rebels see Christians as spiritual slaves and fancy themselves truly free.**

This is an important point to pursue with spiritual rebels. They see Christians as spiritual slaves and fancy themselves truly free. However, if you examine their passions and values, it's not difficult to demonstrate that they too render worship. Our job is to awaken them to the illusion of autonomy. Everybody worships something. Spiritual rebels refuse to bow before God only to end up serving lesser masters.

### "A BETTER FREEDOM"

It's not enough to simply alert spiritual rebels to the illusory freedom of denying God. We need to demonstrate the freedom that comes from serving God. Christian musician Michael Card captures this paradoxical liberty perfectly in his song, "A Better Freedom."

> *A better freedom can't be found*
> *By those unwilling to be bound*
> *A better freedom is not known*
> *By those whose hearts will not be owned*

—MICHAEL CARD

© 2009 Mole End Music, used by permission

The song's lyrics reflect a counterintuitive truth. Surrender brings freedom. Only by submitting to Christ do we escape the tyranny of sin and selfishness. The preacher-poet John Donne used graphic language in begging God for this paradoxical liberty. "Take me to you, imprison me," he wrote, "for I, except you enthrall me, never shall be free, nor ever chaste, except you ravish me." On the surface, Donne's demand seems strange. Why was he so desperate for God's imprisonment? Only because he knew that it was the only way to true freedom: ". . . for I, except you enthrall me, never shall be free."

To reach spiritual rebels, we must model this subversive freedom. I'm convinced that our most powerful witness to them will not come through our words. Rather we will make the greatest impact as we live out a dynamic Christian freedom in their midst. Next to the freedom of those bound by Christ, all other freedoms ring hollow.

# Portrait of a **REBEL**

To her church friends, Jaime seemed like the perfect Christian girl. Growing up she participated in Awana (a sort of Christian version of Girl Scouts), attended her church's Vacation Bible School, and was active in her youth group.

But in high school Jaime started living two lives. "I smoked marijuana, started cutting class, that sort of thing," she recalls. "I just have a rebellious nature, I guess."

Jaime managed to keep her "rebellious nature" secret from the Sunday crowd, even as she wrestled with guilt, and worried about their disapproval. "I didn't want to tell them. I knew they'd look down on me," she says.

When she turned twenty-one, something clicked. She was done living a double life.

"It was a turning point. I just decided I wanted to be young and party and go to clubs, have fun, and mess around with boys. I was done feeling guilty. I felt like I had to be that rebellious person. I couldn't be myself and be a Christian."

Today Jaime is twenty-four, lives with her boyfriend, and has nothing to do with church or her old Christian friends. "I miss the fellowship, but I don't miss getting up really early and being bored to death during the sermon," she says.

There's another reason she stays away. "I don't like the judgment I feel coming from Christians," she explains. "I get a lot of bad feelings from Christians. I think the church is the big downfall of Christianity."

Though she's distanced herself from the church, and doesn't identify as a Christian, she still holds key Christian beliefs. "I believe Jesus was the Son of God, exactly who the Bible says He was," she declares.

She also feels that God is involved in her life. "I feel like He's still got His little bubble around me, protecting me." On the way to a recent job interview, she decided to pray. "I turned off my car radio and just asked God to help me," she said. "I turn to God about big things, when I don't trust my judgment. I still believe, even if my actions don't necessarily reflect that all the time."

Despite her beliefs about God, she bristles at any mention of Christians. "They say Jesus is all loving and stuff, but then if I go out and drink on a Saturday, they're like sobbing about it. There's too much 'obey or go to hell.'"

Jaime wishes Christians would focus more on her and less on her behavior.

"If I tell you that I got drunk, and got herpes—I don't have herpes, but if that were the case—I wouldn't want you to preach at me or say that you'll pray for me, or ask, 'Have you read your Bible?' I just want you to listen to me and be my friend."

# Section 6

---

Drifters

# 15- Meet a Drifter

I want to introduce you to the last kind of leaver in a slightly different way.

We'll start with the story of "Jenny." Jenny is not a person I interviewed. In fact, she is not even a real person but rather a composite of several leavers I have known. However, I believe her story mirrors the experience of countless young people. These are the ones whose faith is rooted in shallow soil and is ultimately carried off in the wind. These are the slow-motion leavers. They don't exit in sudden spasms of skepticism or rebellion. Instead they leave gradually, almost imperceptibly. They also number in the thousands, if not millions, so we've saved the largest group for last.

I call them "Drifters."

## JENNY'S JOURNEY

Jenny was popular in high school, and it wasn't hard to see why. Tall, athletic, and pretty, she was the kind of girl who would be easy to envy—if she wasn't so nice. Each person who passed her in the hall received a warm smile, no matter their place in the adolescent pecking order. When Jenny was voted homecoming queen her senior year, students began mouthing her name before the principal could even read the announcement.

Her family was upper-middle class—at least that's how they preferred to think of themselves. In truth, they were upper-upper class. Jenny's father earned a multiple six-figure income, which was almost superfluous after the death of Jenny's grandmother left the family with a large inheritance.

They attended a nondenominational church near their house in the suburbs. On most Sundays Jenny's mother drove her and her younger brother to church, since her father was usually away on business. At home they rarely discussed spiritual matters. Mentions of God and Jesus came only in the perfunctory family prayers mumbled before dinner. Yet at the same time, it was understood that faith was important. And church was an essential part of living a good life.

Though Jenny attended Sunday morning services regularly, her real connection to church was through youth group. Several of her basketball teammates were members of the youth group as well. The fun they had on Friday nights in the church gymnasium felt like a continuation of the good times they had together throughout the week.

Jenny said a prayer to accept Jesus when she was twelve years old at a summer Bible camp. For her thirteenth birthday her parents gave her a *Student Bible* with her name embossed in gold on the black leather cover. She didn't read it regularly. But after a breakup or a bad game, she would flip it open to the Psalms. That's where her youth pastor instructed her to read when she was feeling down. It was good advice. Reading the poetic cadences always made her feel better. Before big tests and big games she paused to pray silently. It was the same prayer every time. She felt that if she deviated from the ritual that somehow it wouldn't work. "Dear Lord, please help me to focus and perform to the best of my abilities. In Jesus' name. Amen."

One summer, Jenny traveled with the youth group to attend "Aflame!" a Christian youth rally in a neighboring city. When they arrived at the stadium, Jenny was awed. Sixteen thousand teenagers flooded the arena, and busloads more arrived every hour. At the center of the arena was a massive cruciform stage where four cute guys with faux hawks kicked off the three-day festival by strumming and drumming the crowd into a veritable frenzy. Jenny and her friends rushed down to the floor to cheer. Each night they collapsed onto their hotel beds, exhausted from dancing.

The weekend was a swirl of emotions, and Jenny was encountering a new breed of Christian. They raised their hands. They cried. They sang passionately, not just about Jesus, but directly to Him. The atmosphere was powerful, and soon Jenny found herself joining in. On the last night of the festival, a famous preacher took the stage. "Jesus died for you," the preacher said, "the least you can do is live for Him!"

At the end of his sermon he shouted, "Who is ready to live for Jesus?!"

Thousands of teenage voices, including Jenny's, thundered back, "We are!"

After the talk, Jenny was surprised to discover that her face was wet with tears. A flash of embarrassment shot through her as she imagined others seeing her this way, raising her hands and crying, such overt spiritual expressions. But it was dark. Besides, everyone else was doing the same thing.

Jenny returned on a spiritual high. The following Friday she volunteered to share at youth group. She talked about how amazing the weekend was, and how much God had done in her life.

"Things will be different for me from now on," she told the group.

For a few weeks things were different. She told her parents that she had "rededicated her life to Christ." They were approving, if a little perplexed. She also started praying more and reading her Bible every night before bed. She would flip open the Bible and start reading wherever her gaze would fall. At first it was just because she didn't know where to start, but after a couple weeks it turned into a game. "What do you want to say to me today, God?" she would pray, before popping the Bible open and pointing. Often she landed on an obscure verse from Leviticus, or some other verse from an Old Testament book and questioned whether God was really directing her. But other times the verse she flipped to seemed to speak directly and powerfully to her situation. On some nights she kept flipping until she found a passage that applied.

When basketball season started in the fall, she dropped her evening Bible-reading routine. Practice left her too tired to read at the end of the day. And she wasn't feeling as inspired as she did in the days after the youth rally even when she was at church. The sunlight that spilled through the large windows of the sanctuary seemed to erase any excitement she'd felt in the dark cavernous stadium of the youth rally. She passed the services daydreaming or passing notes with a friend during the sermons, which always seemed to be about adult topics anyway. *Who cares about "what the Bible says about family"?* she thought to herself.

The next year Jenny left for college. She was apprehensive. The college was two states away from home, too far to drive back for weekends. She was on her own. Despite her initial apprehension, her outgoing personality quickly drew a new circle of friends around her. It was a different crowd, though, than the one back home. For one thing, only one of her newfound friends identified themselves as a Christian, and she was the wildest one in the bunch. Not that Jenny minded too much. She was happy to be able to sleep in on Sunday mornings and slightly relieved to break free of the good-girl expectations that came with being her high school's most visible overachiever. This group would help her loosen up. One of her college friends supplied her with a fake ID, and she started going to the clubs and partying on the weekends. One night a friend grabbed her by the arm and pulled her off the dance floor. "Take this," she said and extended an open hand to Jenny. In her hand was a pill, Easter-egg blue and no bigger than a baby aspirin. It was Ecstasy.

A few minutes after swallowing the little pill, Jenny's face flushed and she started to sweat. She had an intense feeling of euphoria and love for everything and everyone around her. Her inhibitions evaporated. She danced unself-consciously and spoke freely and deeply with friends and strangers alike. The next morning she marveled at the experience but felt emotionally spent. The day after that she dipped into depression. And she felt guilty. What would her friends back home think? How about her parents? But what made her feel especially ashamed was the thought that she was wasting her potential. She wasn't the kind of girl who did drugs. She never did them again.

In her second term of college, Jenny started dating a senior. At one point, she mentioned something about her church back home.

"You're a Christian?" her boyfriend asked.

"Yes," Jenny replied weakly.

He scowled.

"Well, let me warn you, most Christians on campus are losers. Bunch of Jesus freaks. Besides, haven't you heard?" He laughed. "God's dead. You'll see what I mean if you take philosophy."

Jenny was embarrassed and quickly changed the topic. Later that week she spotted some tables set up in the campus square. A group of Christian students were handing out literature and trying to talk to people about God. Some hurled insults at them as they passed the table. When Jenny saw what was happening, she secretly vowed that she would never be on the receiving end of such public humiliation. In classes the professors openly ridiculed Christian beliefs, and they were the smartest people she had ever met. Jenny started to doubt that anything she'd learned in church was true. But she didn't feel any hostility. Being a good person and reaching your potential—those are what really matter, she thought to herself. She had learned that in church, and she was grateful. The other stuff wasn't all that important.

In her sophomore year, Jenny moved in with her boyfriend. She never went to church, except to please her parents when she went home for holidays, and her old Bible still sat beside the night table in her old room. Most significantly, Jenny never thought about God. She didn't pray. She never talked about her faith. And she didn't care. Jenny was still the nice, outgoing girl everyone loved in high school. But one thing was clear: she wasn't a Christian.

# 16- Why Drifters Leave

There's one thing I'll never understand, no matter how much I read the Old Testament—why the Israelites kept drifting away from God.

Just think about all the supernatural things they witnessed: the parting of the Red Sea, manna from heaven, water from a rock, the guiding cloud and pillar of fire, the Ark of the Covenant, the myriad miracles done through Moses. I could go on.

Yet after having all of these vivid encounters with the living God, after repeatedly receiving His provision and beholding His power, what do they do? Carve up wood or melt down metal and make idols to worship. Devotion wanes. I understand that. But it seems that after seeing such irrefutable displays of the supernatural they would at least obey out of fear, if nothing else.

I'm probably being a little hard on the Israelites. As baffling as their behavior appears, I've glimpsed the same tendency in my own life. I haven't witnessed seas divide or eaten manna from heaven, but I've experienced God.

And I've forgotten. I haven't bowed before idols of wood and stone, but I've opted for petty pleasures over intimacy with the living God. We all have. Unfortunately, it's part of the human condition. "Prone to wander" was how the hymnist put it. Spiritual amnesia, others have said. It's that entrenched human defect—the tendency to drift from God.

## THE ENEMY WITHIN

What's the biggest threat to Christianity?

Twenty years ago, the answer for many Christians seemed obvious: the New Age movement. The voguish blend of eastern mysticism and self-help psychology seemed unstoppable. It was a potent elixir for a culture driven by novelty and narcissism.

As a child growing up in the 1980s, I thought a New Age takeover was likely if not inevitable. As more and more Christians were swept away by the movement, I heard ominous rumblings. Was this the grand deception promised in Revelation that would deceive "even the elect"? Low-budget end times films (and there were many) portrayed showdowns between a faithful remnant of Christians and an antichrist who sounded like a sinister version of Shirley MacLaine, spouting New Age aphorisms while plotting world domination.

Today the New Age movement, though still pervasive, doesn't seem the juggernaut it did then. So what's the biggest threat to the faith today? Well, pick your poison. It could be the kind of militant atheism or earth-based spirituality that we have discussed in previous chapters. Or maybe radical Islam. Or perhaps just regular old Islam, which thanks to a high birthrate among adherents, continues to grow at an astounding rate around the globe.

But if we're honest, I think we'll admit that none of these constitutes the greatest threat to our faith. In fact, the biggest challenge isn't any dark and gathering force beyond the walls of the church. Instead the biggest danger to Christianity is Christians. It's nothing external. It's us! It's that's age-old tendency to drift from God, to lose our first love. The biggest threat to Israel wasn't the Philistines or the Babylonians; it was their fatal propensity to abandon Yahweh. We're no different.

**The biggest danger to Christianity is Christians.**

When we look at those who walk away from the faith, it's essential to understand that this dynamic is at play. They're not so unlike us. The difference between me and my friends who I now describe as "ex-Christians" may be a matter of degree, rather than kind. We all have the tendency to stray. But God, in His mercy, keeps drawing me back and refreshing my love for Him. When I look at those who have left the faith, I have to confess with awe and humility, "There, but for the grace of God, go I."

And yet there are some predictable patterns in the lives of drifters, and looking back, some clear signals they were vulnerable to defection. Whether they were ever really Christians is debatable, but clearly, the faith was never core-deep. Over the preceding chapters, we've explored a wide range of reasons that young people leave. We've examined intellectual crises, psychological traumas, competing worldviews, and even rebellious natures. Many of these factors result in a sharp disjuncture. Young people with such experiences leave the faith, often abruptly, feeling angry, hurt, or liberated. They leave shaking the dust from their feet.

Drifters are different. They exit through a different door—and they don't slam it on their way out. Their journey away from the faith is not sudden or dramatic, perhaps because, like Jenny's it wasn't all that deep in the first place. When they leave you hardly notice. You just wake up one day and realize that they're gone.

## SONS OF "NONE"

In March 2009 the American Religious Identification Survey released the findings of its survey of religious identification in the United States.[1] The 2008 survey was massive; 54,461 Americans were randomly selected and interviewed. If the findings weren't a wake-up call for the church, they should have been. Among the many conclusions of the study, one stood out, headlining news articles and lighting up the blogosphere. The percentage of Americans claiming "no religion" had almost doubled, climbing from 8.1 percent in 1990 to 15 percent in 2008. The trend wasn't confined to one region of the country. The "Nones," as the media called them, was the only group to have risen in every state of the union, from the secular Northeast to the conservative Bible Belt.

But the story of the "Nones" wasn't complete. Later in 2009 the same researchers released a follow-up report that looked at this growing category more closely.[2] The Nones were found to be far more numerous among young Americans than in the general population. Fully 22 percent of eighteen- to twenty-nine-year-olds claimed no religion, up 11 percent from 1990. They also found that 73 percent of Nones came from religious homes, and 66 percent were "deconverts."

Around the same time, the Pew Forum on Religion and Public Life released its own study, *Faith in Flux: Changes in Religious Affiliation in the U.S.* It found the percentage of Nones in the country to be even higher (17 percent). The survey also probed the specific "reasons for leaving childhood religion." Those raised as

Protestants selected a number of reasons for leaving their faith: unhappy with teachings about the Bible (36 percent), spiritual needs not being met (39 percent), stopped believing in the religion's teaching (50 percent). But the reason most often cited (respondents could choose more than one reason) had nothing to do with dissatisfaction with beliefs or practices. Almost three out of four who departed their childhood religion, 71 percent, reported that they "just gradually drifted away from the religion."

## INVISIBLE DRIFT

If you Google the phrase "Why I left Christianity" you will receive about 140 million results. Scan through the pages of results and you'll find provocative site titles such as, "Debunking Christianity," "Christianity's Imminent Downfall," and "Why the Christian god does not exist."

As you might expect, such sites serve as outlets for leavers to mount attacks against the Christian faith, and dialogue with other like-minded people. There are reams of reverse apologetic sites. The next most popular kind of site is the ex-Christian forum. In these online spaces, fellow leavers share ideas, vent frustration, and exchange war stories from their times in the Christian world.

If you were to judge why people leave the faith based solely on such Internet searches, you'd get an overwhelming impression. The vast majority, you would have to conclude, left for intellectual reasons. Furthermore, you'd surmise that most leavers were passionate, even angry about the faith they'd left behind.

But would you be right?

Only partially. You would have learned about a certain kind of leaver—the kind that takes the time and effort to go online and write about the decision to leave the Christian faith. And you'd be correct in concluding that this particular type of leaver has intellectual doubts and strong, negative feelings about Christianity. The problem with this impression is that you would be dealing with what researchers call a "self-selecting pool." In other words, the kind of person who writes about their experience is also the kind of person who is likely to have left for the reasons mentioned above. In fact, as you scan online deconversion testimonies, you'll notice that the same names surface again and again. This vocal minority creates a perception that all those who leave the faith are like them. But these people aren't necessarily representative of other leavers, the ones too busy or apathetic to air their opinions in cyberspace. Among these other kinds of leavers are Drifters. They are the ones who reported "just gradually drifting away," not in forums they sought out, but in randomized surveys conducted by professional researchers.

Drifters don't seek out opportunities to argue against Christianity. In fact, they may not have arguments at all. This might sound like good news for Christians wanting to reach them. After all, there aren't as many emotional and intellectual hurdles to overcome. But Drifter apathy is a double-edged sword. Since Drifters have few intellectual objections to Christianity, they aren't as motivated to open up about their beliefs. They may find conversations about God awkward, and seek to avoid spiritual topics altogether.

Worse yet, since Drifters leave the faith gradually, many don't think they ever even left. They are what might be described as nominal (name-only) Christians. They still identify as Christians, despite the fact that their lives in no way reflect commitment to Christ. Ask a Drifter if she's a Christian, and she'll often answer in the affirmative, blithely accepting the label because she was christened as a baby or muttered a prayer in her teens.

How can we reach Drifters? In the next chapter we'll take a closer look at this unique kind of leaver. We'll also look at the dynamics of Jenny's story and the complex but common set of circumstances that pulled her away from faith. By doing so, we'll discover some effective ways to call Drifters back.

# 17 - Turning the Tide

When Christian Smith and his fellow researchers examined the spiritual lives of American teenagers, what they found shocked the ministry world. It wasn't the revelation that teens are inarticulate about faith (anyone who has worked with teens might have guessed as much) or that teens often fail to grasp even the most basic tenets of their faith. Rather it was Smith's description of the very fabric of teen spirituality that raised eyebrows. Smith defined the religion of most American teenagers, especially Protestant and Catholic teens, as "Moralistic Therapeutic Deism (MTD)," a clunky term that nevertheless quickly entered the lexicon of youth ministers across the country.

What exactly is MTD? Smith breaks it down into five beliefs.

1. "A god exists who created and ordered the world and watches over human life on earth."
2. "God wants people to be good, nice, and fair to each other, as taught in the Bible and by most world religions."
3. "The central goal of life is to be happy and to feel good about oneself."
4. "God does not need to be particularly involved in one's life except when God is needed to resolve a problem."
5. "Good people go to heaven when they die."[1]

Of course not all of these beliefs are unscriptural: The first echoes the Genesis creation account, and the second, the Golden Rule. However, the others hardly resemble Christian teaching. If most young Christians believe life's central goal is to build self-esteem and feel happy, we are in deep trouble. Same goes for the view of God as divine bellhop or the belief that good works secure access to heaven. Such views are self-serving, coldly utilitarian, and bear little resemblance to the holy, personal God revealed in the Bible. It's also a tremendously superficial and fragile faith. Unfortunately, if researchers like Smith are correct, it's exactly the kind of faith many young Christians practice today. No wonder they fall away.

Remember Jenny from chapter 16? You may have recognized several features of MTD in Jenny's story. Jenny's kindness to her fellow students reflects her belief that people be "good, nice, and fair to each other." Similarly, Jenny's tendency to turn to God only when she needs help with games or tests aligns perfectly with belief in a deity who exists primarily for solving problems. She's also focused on self-actualization as life's highest aim. Even when Jenny does drugs, the guilt she feels is not conviction of sin. What made her feel badly was "the thought that she was wasting her potential" by doing drugs. It is MTD to the core.

Like Jenny, most Drifters practiced a faith that fits Smith's definition. Their faith was deeply colored by moral therapeutic deism. I think this is important to understand as we explore ways to reach them.

## JESUS FOR JESUS' SAKE

In the nineteenth century, there was a movement that came to be known as "art for art's sake." Proponents of this philosophy rejected the conventional view that art needed to serve a practical purpose or appeal to a classical ideal. In their eyes, art had intrinsic value, regardless of whether or not it contributed anything practical to society. Art was its own justification for creating art.

This view of art is debatable. Yet I appreciate the idea behind it. When you truly love something, it purifies your motives. Instead of loving it for its practical benefits, you are compelled by love of the thing itself.

It's the same with people. When it comes to Jesus, we definitely have someone worthy of our unqualified devotion. By loving Jesus for Jesus' sake, not only do we fulfill our calling as Christians, we also serve as a powerful example for Drifters. Since Drifters usually practiced a brand of MTD, Christianity was all about what was in it for them. Jesus was a genie in the sky, a power invoked to get them out of a pinch or bring personal gain. When they see us loving Jesus for Jesus' sake—not because we want better things, or even to become a better people—we expose them to an authentic, and more compelling, kind of faith.

## ATMOSPHERE, NOT ARGUMENT

My grandfather, a lifelong pastor, once told me, "People learn spiritual truth through atmosphere, not arguments." Great insight, especially when it comes to understanding Drifters.

As Jenny's story demonstrates, Drifters are easily influenced by environment. They're the kind who blend in, go with the flow. They were likely swept up in the faith in the first place because it was what everyone else around them was doing. Then they left for the same reason. They found themselves in a new context where Christian faith wasn't the norm.

So the first step with Drifters is often to play the role of inviter. Get them into an atmosphere where they can just be around Christians and hear the gospel again. Since Drifters don't tend to have intellectual objections to the faith, you can often bypass apologetics, and just invite them to church and other places where they're likely to encounter other believers and sense the presence of God.

## RAISE THE BAR

But getting them into the right atmosphere is only the first step. They've been there before, and they've left. The problem is that most Drifters grew up in a Christian culture where the hard demands of the gospel weren't properly communicated. Sacrifice and suffering were alien concepts. Instead, they may have received a distinctly MTD type of Christian faith. In order to challenge them to make a complete and lasting commitment to Christ, expose them to the hard demands of the gospel. Emphasize the fact that church isn't merely a social club, and that following Christ is an all-or-nothing proposition.

I remember talking to one Drifter, who had expressed some interest in the faith. After talking about Christianity in theoretical terms for an hour, I stopped the conversation. "Don, I want you to know that this is more than a topic of academic interest for me," I said. "I've staked my life on it. I believe it with my whole heart." That was a turning point in the conversation. By identifying what

Christianity meant for me personally, I opened the door for him to talk about what it could mean for him.

"Do you think that Jesus rose from the dead?" he asked.

"Absolutely," I said.

"If that's true, it would change my life radically," he said. "I mean if Jesus is alive, that means everything is different."

I couldn't have said it better.

## CONNECT

According to Smith's research, one key indicator of whether or not young people stick with their faith was intergenerational connections. Basically, those young people who had relationships to older Christians, whether their parents or other faithful congregants, were far less likely to abandon their faith in their twenties. Again, Jenny's story is telling. Like many teens, her connection to church was almost exclusively through the youth group. And she lacked any deep relationships with Christians outside her age bracket. In the parlance of Christian faith, she was not discipled.

> **Those young people who had relationships to older Christians were far less likely to abandon their faith.**

Many Drifters fall into that category. One of the major reasons they drifted away is because the relational bonds to committed Christians were weak or nonexistent. In order to win them back, we must rectify that destructive isolation. When you bring them to church, seek to widen their circle of Christian friends. Don't let them settle into secluded pockets of the congregation. Introduce them to older Christians, and younger ones. Ask them to serve. Invite them to small groups, prayer meetings, and fellowship times, places where they can grow in the faith and form lasting relationships with mature Christians. And of course, your own example may ultimately be the most powerful tool to see them become passionate followers of Christ. After all, the right steps have been taken, and all the right words uttered, the most compelling witness to God's reality is still a life changed by Him.

# Profile of a DRIFTER

I don't even think about stuff like that."
This was Jake's casual answer when asked about his worldview and thoughts on Christianity. It wasn't because he was intellectually lazy. Jake was intelligent, maybe even a genius. After putting in six years of nonstop work as a Silicon Valley entrepreneur, his Internet company was thriving. It was a small company by Silicon Valley standards, but it was enough to make him wealthy—and keep him busy for just about every waking hour of his life

"There's just no time to think about things other than work. I have way too much to do," he said.

However, busyness wasn't the only thing keeping Jake from mulling spiritual matters. He confessed that his hectic lifestyle also served to shield him from some realities he'd rather not contemplate.

"I intentionally stay away from those kinds of topics," he said. "I don't want to think about death or consider the fact that life could ultimately be meaningless."

Jake didn't always feel that way. He grew up as a

Christian, but felt himself growing cold toward his faith during college. He took some philosophy classes that cast doubt on his beliefs and suffered a bout of depression. But more than anything, his story was one of slow attrition. Once he was away from his family and church, his spiritual life withered and died. Today he doesn't go to church, pray, or read the Bible. And he's honest about his spiritual status.

"I don't consider myself a Christian anymore," he said.

Jake doesn't have strong feelings about the topic, and he doesn't "go there" with Christian family and friends. "They have their beliefs, and I have mine," he says. "We don't discuss it."

What about the other Christians in his life? There aren't any.

"Hey, I live in San Francisco," Jake says. "It's an extremely secular place. This industry I work in is too. I just don't encounter Christians. Well, I probably know some people who are Christians, but they don't talk about it. I guess it's just a personal thing. No one brings it up."

# 18- Come Home!

Ex-Christians pray some of the most beautiful prayers. I only realized this fact when I heeded my wife's advice to start asking one simple question in my interviews. It was an absurd question, really, considering how bitterly most of the people I interviewed had denounced the faith. But I started asking it anyway.

"Do you ever still pray?"

Usually the person's eyes would turn to the ground. If we were talking on the phone, the line would go silent for a few seconds.

"Yes."

"What do those prayers sound like?" I would ask.

That's when they poured out their prayers. They were angry prayers, but beautiful in their honesty and desperation: "God, where are You? Can You hear me? Do You exist? Do You even care about me? I miss You."

One girl told me in a hushed voice about how, on some occasions, she still prays for guidance and for God's protection.

Others breathed prayers of thanksgiving, despite their insistence that there was no one to thank. One example was David Bazan, an indie rock singer who had gradually lost his faith during his mid-twenties.

"One thing I really missed initially when I left the faith was expressing gratitude through prayer," he told me. "So I still say those prayers, just expressing thanks for the beauty of the world and the joy of relationships."

Bazan also missed what he called "the sense of surrender that comes through prayer." He added, "In the parlance of Christianity, I never wanted to have a hard heart." One night, Bazan almost surrendered to God.

"I was lying in bed at night. I just suddenly had that fear: *What if I'm wrong?* I would just lie there terrified, heart pounding. I even started surrendering to God. Then at the last second I just said, 'forget this.'"

In spite of his refusal to turn back to God, he continues to pray.

"Sometimes I still feel like I'm praying to capital G-O-D, and other times I guess I'm just praying to the air."

If those surprising prayers taught me anything, it's that God is still very much at work in the lives of those who have rejected Him. That's heartening. It makes our task of reaching leavers less daunting. Ultimately we don't carry the responsibility to bring them home. That's God's job. Our work involves merely getting behind what He's already doing.

But how can we do that? Let's conclude by taking a brief look at some of the ways we can participate in God's work in their lives.

## DISCOURSE

Wouldn't it be nice if we didn't have to do any homework to reach leavers? If we didn't have to worry about studying up on the arguments for God's existence, the resurrection of Jesus, or the reliability of Scripture?

While that would be easier, it's not reality. We need to know why we believe what we believe. It's essential to our faith and our witness. As we've seen in previous chapters, the arguments we present will vary depending on our audience. But we must be prepared to give good answers to hard questions. Fortunately there are great answers for the questions leavers ask. We just have to do our homework and learn what they are.

At the same time, we shouldn't expect too much from arguments. They're valuable, but have clear limits. It's easy to imagine facing off with ex-Christians in a debate-style format. If we only score enough rhetorical points, we think, we can argue them into the kingdom.

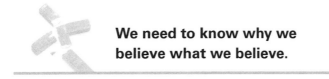

**We need to know why we believe what we believe.**

Of course, that's rarely how it works. Our exchanges with leavers will likely exert a more subtle influence. The impact can be gradual, almost imperceptible. Yet presenting our reasons for God will make a difference, even if we "lose" some arguments. C. S. Lewis wrote, "The very one who argued you down, will sometimes be found, years later, to have been influenced by what you said." I've found this to be true in my own experience. Even when I strongly disagree with someone on a topic, interactions with them affect me. If they present good ideas with clarity and conviction, they often eventually change my mind. We enter into dialogue with leavers with the long view in mind. We're not trying to win arguments. We merely want to clear some of the obstacles to faith. At the very least, we can give them words that will echo in their minds later in life.

## RELATIONSHIP

When I began writing this book, I knew that relationships were important to this issue. However, it wasn't until I talked with dozens of ex-Christians that I realized just how important they really were. Deconversion doesn't happen in a vacuum. A person's decision to abandon the faith is inextricably tied to a host of human connections. The same is true of the decision to come back. In testimony after testimony, we hear of how God uses one or two caring Christians to lead people to Himself. All the words in the world won't matter if we don't forge these kinds of loving relationships with the leavers in our lives.

Of course the relationships between Christians and ex-Christians are notoriously difficult. Conflict is inevitable. It's easy to become discouraged, especially when an ex-Christian seems so hostile to the faith. But take heart. The ones seemingly most resistant to God can be the ones most likely to come home. It's often said that the opposite of love is not hate, but indifference. Emotional reactions to God, even negative ones, are signs of life. Often those who are seemingly beyond God's grace are those who are actually closest to returning.

## PRAYER

In the moment that Andrew Palau finally surrendered to God, he was hit with a distinct impression. He described it like a voice in his head: *Do you realize how many prayers went up to make this possible?* There were dozens, perhaps hundreds, of Christians faithfully petitioning God for his return. When that moment of surrender came, God impressed upon him the crucial role that those prayers played.

It's impossible to overstate the importance of prayer. I'm convinced that we can give our loved ones who have strayed no greater gift than time spent in the presence of God on their behalf. Plead, ramble, cry, rage—but don't stop. We can be confident that when we pray for prodigals, we are praying according to God's will. Our desire to see them return is nothing next to His.

In the introduction to this book I described a famous painting that depicts a shepherd reaching over a cliff to rescue his lost sheep. I wondered if there was a single image to better convey the desire of God to see His lost sheep return.

It now occurs to me that there is a better image. It too is of a Shepherd, not on a cliff, but on a cross. His arms reach, not over a precipice, but across the distance of a rough-hewn cross. It is here that the Good Shepherd makes His most passionate appeal, even to those who reject Him. It's not too late to return, He seems to say. My arms are still open. The offer still stands. Come home!

# Appendix

## Won't They Come Back
# When They're Older?

A few recent books suggest that the bleak statistics about young people leaving the church are misleading, and that reaction to the trend has been overblown. Sociologist of religion Rodney Stark is one of those calling for calm. The Baylor professor concedes that data from his school's study show a sharp drop-off in church participation, but Stark isn't shaken by such findings. "Young people have always been less likely to attend than are older people," he says.[1]

Furthermore, Stark remains confident that young people will return to the church a few years down the road. "A bit later in life when they have married, and especially after children arrive, they become more regular attenders. This happens in every generation."[2]

Stark is correct in noting that young people have always had the highest church dropout rates. We shouldn't be surprised by this phenomenon. After all, during young adulthood many changes are afoot. Young adults leave their parents' homes and go to college. They move repeatedly.

They start and quit jobs. They strike up new romances. They launch careers. Amid this flurry of transition and activity, a dip in church attendance is almost guaranteed. According to some forecasters, when this period of transition slows, they will resume the churchgoing habits of their early years.

The case of the Baby Boomers is instructive. Though many left the church in the sixties and seventies, millions have returned in the last twenty-plus years, swelling suburban churches across the country.

## MEET THE NEW YOUNG ADULTS

I'd love to share Stark's optimism. Unfortunately, there are unique factors that I believe make this generation different. First, young adults today are dropping their faith at a greater rate than those of yesteryear. Reporting on the latest studies, Harvard professor Robert Putnam and Notre Dame professor David Campbell report: "Young Americans are dropping out of religion at an alarming rate of five to six times the historic rate (30–40% have no religion today versus 5–10% a generation ago)."[3] Comparing today's young people with their parents, may be like comparing apples and oranges.

Second, young adulthood is not what it used to be. For one, it's longer. Much longer. Notre Dame sociologist Christian Smith describes this new extended phase in life. "The transition from the teenage years to fully achieved adulthood has stretched out into an extended stage that is often amorphous, unstructured, and convoluted, lasting upward of twelve or more years."[4]

Journalists have called those caught in this long-drawn-out period of life a host of new names, including Adultolescents, Twixters, and Emerging Adults. During this time, young adults postpone careers, delay marriage, and put off having children. Previous generations also had to navigate the turbulent waters of the young adult years. The difference is that for them, this phase typically lasted a few years. For today's young people, it often lasts more than twelve years.

This protracted time of rootless living hardly encourages consistent religious involvement. Historically, getting married and having children have been the most powerful draws for young people to come back to church. But with the average age of marriage stretching into the late twenties, and many opting to put off having children (or deciding to have none at all), some of the most potent motivators to return to church life are evaporating.

The delay may radically decrease the chance that they will one day return to church at all. Returning to the fold after a two- or four-year hiatus is one thing. Coming back after more than a decade absence is considerably more difficult. With each passing year that young adults stay away from the church, the odds that they will ever return diminish significantly.

Smith has done some of the most in-depth studies of the spiritual lives of young people. He and fellow Notre Dame sociologist Patricia Snell interviewed hundreds of teenagers from forty-two states and then followed their spiritual development into their twenties. When it comes to maintaining long-term faith commitments, Smith sees two determinate factors. The first involves parents. The children of parents who model a dynamic faith are more likely to stick with the faith. In an interview with *Christianity Today*, Smith stated: "For better or worse, parents are tremendously important in shaping their children's faith trajectories."[5]

The second factor is teenage devotion. According to Smith, those who "established devotional lives—that is, praying, reading Scripture—during the teenage years . . . are much more likely than those who don't to continue doing so into emerging adulthood."

Smith himself is circumspect when it comes to assessing the

role an extended young adulthood will ultimately have on the faith of young adults. He conceded that "most of what happens in emerging adulthood works against serious faith commitments." Yet he stated that "for some emerging adults, the chaos (of this life phase) helps them find that religion is an extremely helpful antidote." However, Smith was quick to qualify this second possibility, adding that "only some look to faith to provide stability; most do not go there in the first place."

Some people hold out hope for a mass return, insisting that most young adults who leave church nevertheless retain their faith. Again Baylor's Stark is optimistic. He does not see belief changes behind the high dropout rate. So what's his explanation for the current, large-scale exodus from churches?

> What this persistent finding actually reveals is far more mundane than the notion that young people are leaving the churches. It merely shows that when young people leave home, some of them tend to sleep in on Sunday morning rather than go to church.[6]

I wish I could agree with Stark. It would be comforting for me as a Christian to believe that young people are simply slapping the snooze on Sunday mornings. Unfortunately, I fear that many of those who stay home on Sunday mornings have also abandoned core Christian beliefs and practices.

## THE "INTERNAL-WITHOUT-EXTERNAL" THEORY OF RELIGION

Smith's studies on the religion of young adults prompted him to address a widely held theory about young people's religious beliefs. He calls it the "internal-without-external religion theory."

There is a widespread belief that, as teenagers grow into emerging adults, they tend to drop out of public, external expressions of faith—like religious service attendance and other religious group participation—but that their religious faith nevertheless remains highly valued and vital in their private, subjective, internal lives.[7]

In other words, many commentators hold the belief that young people who do not participate in religious activities still maintain their inner religious convictions. Smith writes that this view is "commonly assumed in both the popular imagination and in some scholarly works." This idea, Smith notes, corresponds with the assumption that these inwardly pious young people will eventually make their way back to more public, corporate expressions of faith.

The implication is often that what "really" matters about religion—interior personal commitment—is in fact well established and secured during the emerging adult years, that it is only the external "trappings" of religious practice that decline during this life phase. Many of them, it is presumed, will in due time—with marriage and children—bring their levels of external religious participation back up to match their allegedly higher levels of continuously sustained internal religious commitment and importance.[8]

There's only one problem with this view. As Smith writes, the "internal-without-external religion" theory turns out to be a myth. He concludes, "Little evidence supports the idea that emerging adults who decline in regular external religious practice nevertheless retain over time high levels of subjectively important, privately committed, internal religious faith. Quite the contrary is indicated by our research."[9]

That is to say, those who stopped going to church, also stopped praying, studying the Bible, and over time, quite possibly stop believing and practicing their faith altogether. There are myriad exceptions to this rule; not all who leave the church leave the faith. There is even a minority movement of young Christians who have left formal church in search of a more pristine faith. But those are the exceptions. For the vast majority, leaving the church is a decisive first step on the path away from faith. It may be comforting to view their departure as a temporary hiatus and assume that most young people will automatically return en masse. I pray that they will. Unfortunately, such thinking may do more harm than good by giving us false hope and luring us into complacency.

# Notes

**Chapter 1: Good-bye, God**

1. Thom Rainer and Sam. S. Rainer III, *Essential Church* (Nashville: B&H Publishing, 2008), 4.
2. David Kinnaman, *UnChristian* (Grand Rapids: Baker Books, 2007), 23.
3. http://hookedongrace.wordpress.com/2007/05/16/but-teenagers-scare-me/
4. James V. Schall, *The Collected Works of G.K. Chesterton* (San Francisco: Ignatius, 1987), 23.

**Chapter 2: Reality Remix**

1. C. S. Lewis, *Mere Christianity*, 3rd ed. (New York: Harper, 2001), 52.
2. http://www.christianitytoday.com/outreach/articles/starbucksspirituality.html
3. http://www.washingtonpost.com/wp-dyn/articles/A21050-2004Oct9.html
4. http://www.christianitytoday.com/ct/2000/november13/8.76.html

**Chapter 3: Welcoming Back Postmodern Leavers**

1. David Kinnaman, *UnChristian* (Grand Rapids: Baker, 2007), 74–75.
2. Ibid., 74.
3. http://www.campuscrusade.com/fourlawseng.htm
4. David Kinnaman, *UnChristian* (Grand Rapids: Baker, 2007), 72.

5. http://www.christianitytoday.com/ct/2005/november/19.128.html
6. Don Everts and Doug Schaupp, *I Once Was Lost* (Downers Grove, Ill.: InterVarsity, 2008), 15.
7. Ibid., 30–31.
8. http://www.christianitytoday.com/outreach/articles/starbucks spirituality.html
9. Ibid.

**Chapter 5: Recoilers**

1. From an interview I conducted with Marjorie Gunnoe.
2. From an interview I conducted with Marjorie Gunnoe.
3. http://www.merriam-webster.com/dictionary/MARRIAGE
4. Annette Mahoney and colleagues, "Religion and the Sancification of Family Relationships," *Review of Religious Research*, 2003, Vol 44:3, 220–36.
5. From an interview I conducted with Edward Shafranske.
6. "Stumbling Blocks on the Religious Road: Fractured Relationships, Nagging Vices, and the Inner Struggle to Believe," *Psychological Inquiry*, 2002. Vol 13, No. 3, 182–89.
7. "Stumbling Blocks on the Religious Road: Fractured Relationships, Nagging Vices, and the Inner Struggle to Believe," *Psychological Inquiry*, 2002. Vol 13, No. 3, 182–89.

**Chapter 6: Reaching Recoilers**

1. From an interview I conducted with Marjorie Gunnoe.
2. From an interview I conducted with Edward Shafranske.

**Chapter 7: Dawkins Disciples**

1. http://ctlibrary.com/ct/2001/julyweb-only/7-23-22.0.html?email=ddyck@christianityto-day.com&password=drew&login=true&x=0&y=0.
2. http://petitions.number10.gov.uk/freethinking/
3. http://www.answersingenesis.org/about/faith

**Chapter 8: Modern Man**

1. http://www.probe.org/site/c.fdKEIMNsEoG/b.4415423/

**Chapter 9: Speaking to Modern Leavers**

1. Donald Miller, *Blue Like Jazz* (Nashville: Nelson, 2003), 103.

2. Sean McDowell, editor, *Apologetics for a New Generation* (Eugene, Oreg.: Harvest House, 2009), 16.
3. http://www.biblio.com/isbn/9781573921473.html

## Chapter 10: Wicca's Spell

1. *Generation Hex: Understanding the Subtle Dangers of Wicca* (Eugene, Oreg.: Harvest House, 2008, 233.
2. http://www.catherinesanders.com/writings/breakpoint051028.html
3. NPR broadcast, *New Religion in America: Alternative Movements Gain Ground with Flexibility, Modernity* by Barbara Bradley Hagerty.
4. Michael Howard, *Modern Wicca: A History from Gerald Gardner to the Present* (Llewellyn, 2009), 1.
5. Rodney Stark and William Bainbridge, *The Future of Religion* (Berkeley, Calif.: Univ. of California, 1986), 445.
6. Catherine Sanders, *Wicca's Charm* (Colorado Springs: WaterBrook Multnomah, 2005), 168.

## Chapter 13: Rebels

1. Faith in Flux: Changes in Religious Affiliation in the U.S. Pew Forum on Religion and Public Life, April, 2009. http:"pewforum.org/Faith-in-Flux.aspx

## Chapter 14: Rebels Needing a Cause

1. http://www.christianchronicle.org/article814~Is "Halo_3"_a_tool_for_outreach_or_a_bad_influence%3F

## Chapter 16: Why Drifters Leave

1. http://www.americanreligionsurvey-aris.org/reports/highlights.html
2. http://www.americanreligionsurvey-aris.org/reports/NONES_08.pdf

## Chapter 17: Turning the Tide

1. Christian Smith, *Soul Searching: The Religious and Spiritual Lives of American Teenagers* (Oxford, England: Oxford University Press, 2005), 162–63.

## Appendix: Won't They Come Back When They're Older?

1. Rodney Stark, *What Americans Really Believe* (Waco, Tex.: Baylor Univ. Press, 2008), 196.
2. Ibid.

3. William McKenzie, "Why are Millennials Dropping Out?" Religion Blog, *The Dallas Morning News*, March, 2010..

4. Christian Smith and Patricia Snell, *Souls in Transition* (Oxford, England: Oxford Univ. Press, 2009), 280.

5. http://www.christianitytoday.com/ct/2009/october/21.34.html?start=4

6. Stark, *What Americans Really Believe*, 203.

7. Smith and Snell, *Souls in Transition*, 251.

8. Ibid.

9. Ibid., 252

# Acknowledgments

I want to thank the following people for their support. Some of you have contributed directly to this project. All of you have impacted my life. It hasn't gone unnoticed.

Thanks to ...

**My wife, Grace**—Your love, wisdom, encouragement, and editorial input made this book possible. You're the best wife in the world! What are you doing with me again?

**The Fam**—Mom, for passing along a passion for the written word and encouraging me when I started churning out sappy devotionals as a teenager. Dad, for being my spiritual role model, and remaining faithful to God amid a brutal battle with Parkinson's. I'll be happy to be half the man you are. Dan, Darren and David, I love you. I couldn't ask for better big brothers! Grandpa, for your profound spiritual insights and life of service to God, thank you.

**The Keohane clan**—(And yes, that includes you, Jason.) For letting me marry into a great second family. Brian and Jane, thanks for not defriending me on Facebook (or in real life) after any one of our many raucous theological debates. You've taught me a lot.

**Moody Publishers**—For taking a chance on this book. Madison, you championed the project, and patiently guided a first-timer through the process, offering excellent insights along the way. Betsey, thanks for seeing it through to completion. You were both awesome to work with!

**Jericho Road Church**—It's a joy to be part of a congregation with such a passion to reach out and serve the community.

**Coworkers**—The people at Christianity Today International, for your faithfulness and brilliance. I'm blessed to serve alongside you.

**Writer buddies**—Brandon O'Brien, Skye Jethani, David Kopp, Marshall Allen, Margaret Feinberg, and my writers' group at work. You helped this book come together. Thank you!

**The interviewees**—For your willingness to share your stories. You broke my heart but opened my eyes to the journey traveled by so many. Thank you for your honesty. Keep seeking, and let's keep talking.

**Jesus.** It's all about You—and that's more than a song lyric. For saving me, and patiently transforming me to Your likeness, I'll be eternally grateful.

Simply the best guide on the varieties of unbelief in the post-modern era. Not only does *Generation Ex-Christian* compassionately diagnose the ways people flee and fight God, but Drew Dyck wisely counsels his readers on how to best communicate and model the beauty, truth, and compassion of the Gospel to each variety of unbelief. The book captivated me from beginning to end.

—JIM BELCHER, author of *Deep Church*

Drew guides us through the blur of the forest's edge, and crouches down to point out the various root causes of why young people are deserting the Christian faith. By exposing our overgeneralizations, this book helps us to respond with love, truth, and grace one person at a time.

—JAMES CHOUNG, author of *True Story*

Many of us have had the heart-wrenching experience of watching someone we love abandon their walk with God. In fact, young people are leaving the Christian faith at an alarming and unprecedented rate. In this insightful and important book, which I nearly finished in a single sitting, Drew Dyck delves into the reasons for this phenomenon, giving us six different categories of leavers and practical ways to re-engage them. A compelling read for anyone involved with today's youth.

—FELICITY DALE, House2House Ministries and
co-author of *The Rabbit and the Elephant*

As a 20-something I struggle with watching my peers leave the church one-by-one. *Generation Ex-Christian* is a great tool to better understand the needs of young adults. Don't wait for another young person to leave the church. Pick up your copy today!

—RENEE JOHNSON, author of *Faithbook of Jesus* and creator of Throw Mountains.

Every person that leaves the church has a story—it's often complicated and interwoven with a myriad of life experiences. Dyck unwinds these multifaceted stories and carefully explains why young adults drift from God. You will recognize many of Dyck's portraits. They are people in your life—your neighbors, family, and friends. He reveals the emotional backdrop of why people wander from faith. This book will help you find ways to journey with people and help guide them back to the one, true story that matters most.

—SAM RAINER, president of Rainer Research and author of *Essential Church?: Reclaiming a Generation of Dropouts*

What Drew does here is take something that people of faith are often scared to think about, something that people of faith need to think about, and make us face the problem. Then he provides real insight into why young people leave and gives guidance on how to engage them.

—JOSH RIEBOCK, author of mY Generation

Drew Dyck wants to help people who once were found, but now are lost. He paints detailed portraits of those who've left the church and the Christian faith in all their complexity. But he doesn't write as a disinterested documentarian merely cataloguing the reasons for their departures. *Generation Ex-Christian* is ultimately about bringing 'leavers' back to faith. He offers unlikely but welcome counsel in this age of non-judgmental "conversations" and "journeys." If you're longing to rescue friends, relatives, and others who've left their Christian faith, *Generation Ex-Christian* is for you.

—CANDICE WATTERS, founding editor of Boundless.org

# WHY TRUST JESUS?

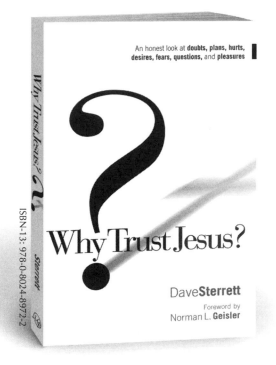

Our generation is up for grabs! Our trust has been shattered in other areas as we have seen hypocrisy in governmental leaders as well as in the church. We are looking for relationships that are authentic and full of life, but we have many questions in regard to faith, reason, suffering and even the person of Jesus himself.

MOODY
PUBLISHERS
moodypublishers.com

# NOT GODS TYPE

What happens when an atheist college professor at spiritual ground zero asks: What if God is real? A young, white, highly educated atheist and professor of English, Holly Ordway represents the kind of person that many observers of religion say cannot be converted anymore. Yet through a series of conversations with a wise and patient mentor, Ordway not only became convinced of God's existence, but also embraced Jesus as her Savior and Lord.

MOODY
PUBLISHERS
moodypublishers.com